Fatalism and the Logic of Time

Fatalism and the Logic of Time

LINDA TRINKAUS ZAGZEBSKI

UNIVERSITY PRESS

OXFORD
UNIVERSITY PRESS

Oxford University Press is a department of the University of Oxford. It furthers the University's objective of excellence in research, scholarship, and education by publishing worldwide. Oxford is a registered trade mark of Oxford University Press in the UK and certain other countries.

Published in the United States of America by Oxford University Press
198 Madison Avenue, New York, NY 10016, United States of America.

© Oxford University Press 2024

All rights reserved. No part of this publication may be reproduced, stored in a retrieval system, or transmitted, in any form or by any means, without the prior permission in writing of Oxford University Press, or as expressly permitted by law, by license, or under terms agreed with the appropriate reproduction rights organization. Inquiries concerning reproduction outside the scope of the above should be sent to the Rights Department, Oxford University Press, at the address above.

You must not circulate this work in any other form
and you must impose this same condition on any acquirer.

CIP data is on file at the Library of Congress

ISBN 978–0–19–778668–0

DOI: 10.1093/oso/9780197786680.001.0001

Printed by Integrated Books International, United States of America

*Dedicated to the memory of Robert Merrihew Adams,
philosophical exemplar and long-time friend*

Contents

Foreword — ix

Introduction — 1

Part One. The (Incoherent) Root of Traditional Fatalist Arguments — 11
  Section 1. Beginning with theological fatalism — 11
    1.1. Our primary argument — 11
    1.2. The Ockhamist idea of accidental necessity — 20
  Section 2. Unraveling theological fatalism — 25
    2.1. First stage: Is the problem uniquely about God's infallibility and fatalism? No. — 25
    2.2. Second stage: Is the problem uniquely about infallibility and fatalism? No. — 34
    2.3. Third stage: Is the problem uniquely about infallibility and time? No. — 40
    2.4. Conclusion to section 2: The incoherence of accidental necessity — 52
  Section 3. Reactions and consequences — 56
    3.1. Can the conclusion be avoided? — 56
    3.2. Conclusion to Part One — 61

Part Two. Fatalism and the Causal Structure of Time — 63
  Section 1. Revisiting the necessity of the past — 63
    1.1. The causal closure of the past and fatalist arguments — 63
    1.2. The consequence argument against determinism — 78
  Section 2. Backward causation and backward counterfactual power — 86
    2.1. Does backward agent causation exist? — 86
    2.2. Counterfactual power over the past — 98
  Section 3. Conclusion to Parts One and Two — 106

Part Three. Does Time Have an Arrow? — 112

Works Cited — 123
Index — 127

Foreword

In 1991 I published my first book, *The Dilemma of Freedom and Foreknowledge* (New York: Oxford University Press), an examination of a problem I had thought about since childhood. Since then, I have come back to the apparent fatalist consequences of divine foreknowledge from time to time, and I resolved to write another book on the subject only if it could be short, simple, and comprehensive. I came to believe that the structural identity of arguments for logical, causal, and theological fatalism press us to examine the arguments together, not only because of our interest in divine foreknowledge, or causal determinism, or the logic of future contingents. Then, several years ago, I got the idea that these arguments have an implication that is even broader than fatalism, and which reveals our confusion about the logic of time. I discussed that briefly in a paper called "Divine Foreknowledge and the Metaphysics of Time," published in 2014 in Munich in a book edited by Anselm Ramelow and reprinted in the collection of my philosophy of religion papers, *God, Knowledge, and the Good* (New York: Oxford University Press, 2022).

Recently, I decided that it was time to put together the thoughts I have developed about fatalism over the last thirty-five years to see if they really can be expressed in a short, uncomplicated book. This book is as short and as simple as I could make it, although the subject matter is remarkably resistant to the simplifying urge. Writing it was fun, and it led to a conclusion I had not anticipated that goes far beyond my worries about fatalism. The book is comprehensive in one sense but not another. It is comprehensive in the sense that the argument leads me into a very wide subject matter, but it is not comprehensive in the sense of doing justice to the major published work on fatalism over the last several decades. I apologize to those philosophers whose work has advanced the discussion during that time but whom I do not mention. This book is an essay, and I hope that it will be read that way. It represents my own intellectual voyage in thinking about fatalism. I begin with a standard fatalist argument and carry it as far as I can. I do not discuss and assess other published material except when that material moved me in the direction I present in the book. If my argument works, I think it is exciting. But in any case, I hope that it will help readers to get insights about time and its logic, and that they will enjoy the journey.

I thank Patrick Todd and an anonymous referee for comments on the entire manuscript, and the students in my final seminar at the University of Oklahoma, when I was working on the ideas in Part One of this book.

Linda Zagzebski
Santa Fe, New Mexico
December 27, 2023

Note on formatting. In this book I have endeavored to follow the convention of italicizing propositions, the bearers of truth value, but not the sentences that express them. Sentence variables are not italicized.

Introduction

From earliest times all over the world there has been a fascination with fatalism. In Greek, fate is *moira*, in Sanskrit, *daiva*, in Chinese, *ming*, in Latin, *fortuna*. What I mean by a fated event is one that is necessitated by something in its past, so when the event occurs, there is no other possibility. If there is no other possibility when an event occurs, it appears to be beyond our control. That is threatening if the event is something we thought we could control, especially if it has life-changing consequences. If every event is fated, we do not control anything in our lives. Of course, we need to accept the fact that we do not have complete control over our lives, but we like to think that we control most of our choices, some of our thoughts, and, to a lesser extent, our emotions. It is up to us to determine the direction of our lives. If that is an illusion, we are not persons but objects.

One form of fatalism that has had special dramatic appeal since antiquity is the Big Fated Event, the kind of fate that an event has when no matter what anybody does, it will happen. If the fated event is good, it is usually called destiny. Aeneas was fated to leave Troy and become the founder of Rome. That was his destiny. In Indian folklore there is an enchanting tale about a poor boy who is destined to marry a princess.[1] Both Aeneas and the Indian boy reach their destinies by a circuitous route, so it is unlikely that the steps to their destiny are fated. Curiously, we do not find destiny frightening even though good fate takes away control just as much

---

[1] "The King Who Would be Stronger than Fate," in Andrew Lang, *The Brown Fairy Book*, http://mythfolklore.net/andrewlang/260.htm.

as bad fate. Instead, we think that the person with a destiny is specially blessed. But if the Big Fated Event is one's undoing by an enemy, as in *Macbeth*, we call that tragic.

An even more poignant version of the Big Fated Event is one in which the belief in the fated event inadvertently brings it about. Sophocles' *Oedipus Rex* and the legendary *Appointment with Death* are stories of that kind.[2] Oedipus' father, Laius, is told by an oracle that his son is fated to kill him. A servant is ordered to kill the baby, but unwilling to do so, he leaves Oedipus on a mountain where he is rescued by a shepherd. When Oedipus grows up, he consults the oracle and learns that he is fated to kill his father and marry his mother. Thinking that the shepherd is his father, he flees, killing his real father on the road and marrying his mother, the queen. Believing the prophecy leads Oedipus and his parents to fulfill it. But what if they had not known it? Would it still have happened but by a different causal path? It is hard to know what Sophocles thought because he did not write another play called *Oedipus in Another Possible World*.

In the *Appointment with Death*, a merchant sends his servant to the marketplace in Baghdad. The servant sees Death beckoning him, and in fear, he runs to his master and pleads, "Lend me your horse so that I can ride to Samarra. I saw Death a moment ago threatening me and I must get away from him." The man lends his servant the horse, and the servant rides off in great haste. The man then sees Death in the marketplace and asks, "Why did you threaten my servant just now?" Death replies, "Oh, I wasn't threatening him. I was just surprised to see him here. I have an appointment with him tonight in Samarra." I imagine that the moral of the stories of Oedipus and the appointment in Samarra is that if something really is your fate, it is not a good idea to try to flee it.

---

[2] This ancient Mesopotamian tale was retold by Somerset Maugham (2007) in his 1933 play, *Sheppey*. It is also the epigraph to John O'Hara's 1934 novel, *Appointment in Samarra*. There are many versions of the story, and it is referenced in the *Babylonian Talmud*, one of the two Talmuds used as the basis for rabbinic law.

The form of fatalism that has always received the most philosophical attention is universal fatalism: Every event is such that something in the past makes it impossible that anything else occurs. That is not always called fatalism since many philosophers deny that determinism is fatalism, yet determinists also say that every event is the only possible event, given the past. But I am interested in any argument for the conclusion that something in the past necessitates the entire future, whether or not it is called "fatalism."

Universal fatalism is worse than the Big Fated Event in one way but less threatening in another. It is more threatening in the sense that it implies that there is nothing in our lives that we control, as opposed to one crucial fated event. But it is less threatening in the sense that no single event is fated more than any other, so fate seems trivial. We still get to do what we decide, but what we decide is fated; our thoughts are fated; our desires our fated. The accumulation of all past fated events makes the entire future fated, and while there may be no single climactic event worthy of being foretold by an oracle, the forces of fate create climactic changes in small steps. Ultimately, every event occurs because of forces in the past.

In mythological societies fate is personified. In Greek mythology the Fates are three goddesses. In Norse mythology the fates are maiden deities called Norns, who visit a child at birth and determine his or her destiny. Some Norns are benevolent; some are malevolent. In the 6th century, the Roman senator and consul Boethius was imprisoned by the emperor Theodoric, and while in prison and afflicted with depression, he wrote his famous work *The Consolation of Philosophy* (1962), which includes the mesmerizing image of the goddess Fortune determining our fate by the turn of a wheel:

> When Fortune turns her wheel with her proud right hand, she is as unpredictable as the flooding Euripus; at one moment she fiercely tears down mighty kings, at the next the hypocrite exalts the humbled captive. She neither hears nor cares about the tears

of those in misery; with a hard heart she laughs at the pain she causes. This is the way she amuses herself; this is the way she shows her power. (Book II, Poem 1, 23)

This is frightening because Fortune has a will and is heartless. She exercises her power ruthlessly, laughs at misery. That is hard to take. But look at the text following Boethius' poem in which Fortune is speaking:

> When nature produced you from your mother's womb, I found you naked and lacking in everything. I nourished you with abundant gifts, and, being inclined to favor you (an attitude which you now seem to hold against me), I endowed you with all the affluence and distinction in my power. Now it pleases me to withdraw my favor. You should be grateful for the use of things which belonged to someone else; you have no legitimate cause of complaint, as though you lost something which was your own. Why then are you so sad? I have done you no injury. Riches, honors, and all good fortune belong to me. They obey me as servants obey their mistress: they come with me, and when I go, they go too. I would even say that, if the things which you complain about losing had really been yours, you would never have lost them. (23–24)

In other words, don't be such a baby. You have no right to complain about your fate. You did not complain when it was good, so why complain when it is bad? "The Lord giveth and the Lord taketh away; blessed be the name of the Lord" (Job 1:21).

It is interesting that there is a difference in the human reaction to fate if it is the product of impersonal nature rather than a person with a will such as a god or a personified Fortune. In Helmut Schoeck's (1966) classic work on envy, he observes that people are more likely to accept fate when it is blind and anonymous rather than the will of a person. In speaking of the early Greek anxiety over fate, Schoeck writes:

To the Greeks of that time it may have seemed very probable that indeed all unequal portions in life were due to the agency of a regulating power that could not be personified. In effect, they felt it better not to visualize too clearly, or imagine in concrete form, the distributor of lots, lest "he" or "she," through the very fact of our thoughts being directed towards the divinity or the conceptually imagined demon, might notice us and begin to wonder what our lot should be. Man feels safest when the distributor of his lot in life remains anonymous, when his fate is, so to speak, what he draws in the lottery. (147)

Impersonal fate is easier to accept. Would anybody blame the deep structure of nature or the nature of God for their fate? The deep structure of the universe cannot respond as Fortune does in Boethius's myth, although perhaps God can do so as he responds to Job if fate is created through the divine will. But if universal fatalism is the result of the truth of propositions about the future, or God's infallible foreknowledge, nobody would blame God for his nature or propositions for their truth value.

However, that does not mean that we like it. The topic of this book is universal fatalism. The dominant reaction to this kind of fatalism from Aristotle to the present is negative. We hope it is not true. I hope it is not true. But that is not universal. In *Living Without Free Will*, Derk Pereboom (2006) argues that according to our best scientific theories, factors beyond our control ultimately determine all our actions, and therefore we are not morally responsible for them. But he points out that if in contrast, our actions exhibited the indeterminacy of quantum events, they would still be produced by factors beyond our control, and again, we would not be responsible for them. The result of the chance turn of the Wheel of Fortune is not fated, but it is just as much out of our control as a fated event. Maybe the goddess Fortune spins her wheel randomly, not knowing herself where it will stop, but if she did so, we would be no more in control of our lives than if she decided to make the wheel stop at a certain spot. So, whether our acts are necessitated or non-necessitated because they are random, we do not have free will. But Pereboom argues that we should not be afraid of the lack of free will. Morality and meaning remain intact in a world without free will. However, I am not ready to accept fatalism, and I will argue that there is something deeply misconceived in standard arguments for fatalism. The failure of common arguments for fatalism does not mean that fatalism is false, but it does mean that these arguments do not force us to find meaning in a fatalistic life.

Why think that fatalism is true? Fatalism dictated by the choice of a personal being is based on myths expressing human concerns that are impervious to reason. Fatalism arising from deep features of the universe supposedly arises from hard reason using apparently irrefutable premises. God's past infallible beliefs about the future seem to logically necessitate the entire future. The principle that every event is caused by past events ultimately leading back to the origin of the universe also seems to necessitate the entire future. Philosophers going back to the ancient Greeks have worried that the past truth of propositions about the future necessitates the entire future. Since the Greeks were both myth makers and probably the earliest people to make reason primary, they had to contend with both kinds of reasons. But fatalism arising from the force of logic is much harder to deny than the personified Fortune of Boethius' tale or the Greek Fates. We feel that we have some control when we interact with a person; maybe we can bargain with them. But we have no control over the force of logic. It is what it is.

I will address universal fatalism—the theory that everything happens out of necessity. There are three historically important forms of it that have the same structure and are all forms of the same problem in the logic of time. *Logical fatalism* is the position that the truth of propositions about the future entails fatalism. *Theological fatalism* is the position that God's infallible knowledge of the future entails fatalism. *Causal fatalism* is the position that the state of the world in the distant past in conjunction with the laws of nature entails fatalism.

Each argument gets its force from the combination of two common principles. One is the principle of the necessity of the past, which we can loosely express as the principle that the past is fixed and beyond anyone's control. Initially I will call that now-necessity. The other is a transfer of necessity principle, the principle that if *p* is necessary in some sense or other, and *p* entails *q*, then *q* is necessary in the same sense as *p*. Both principles deserve much further clarification and discussion, but at the outset we can see how they are the key premises in all three fatalist arguments, and so they will require our attention in what follows.

Short argument for logical fatalism

(1) The proposition *S will occur tomorrow* was true in the past. (Assumption)
(2) It is now-necessary that (1). (Necessity of the past)
(3) (1) entails that S will occur tomorrow. (Definition of "true")
(4) If it is now-necessary that (1), and if (1) entails that S will occur tomorrow, then it is now-necessary that S will occur tomorrow. (Transfer of Necessity Principle)
(5) Therefore, it is now-necessary that S will occur tomorrow. (2, 3, 4)
(6) So, S is fated. It will occur out of necessity.

Short argument for theological fatalism

(1) God infallibly believed in the past *S will occur tomorrow*. (Assumption)
(2) It is now-necessary that (1). (Necessity of the past)

8 FATALISM AND THE LOGIC OF TIME

(3) (1) entails that S will occur tomorrow. (Definition of infallibility)
(4) If it is now-necessary that (1), and if (1) entails that S will occur tomorrow, then it is now-necessary that S will occur tomorrow. (Transfer of Necessity Principle)
(5) Therefore, it is now-necessary that S will occur tomorrow. (2, 3, 4)
(6) So, S is fated. It will occur out of necessity.

Short argument for causal fatalism

Let H = a proposition expressing the total past history of the world, L = a proposition expressing universal causal laws. Assume causal determinism: H and L entails the truth of all future events.

(1) H and L was true in the past. (Assumption)
(2) It is now-necessary that (1). (Necessity of the past)
(3) (1) entails that S will occur tomorrow. (Thesis of causal determinism)
(4) If it is now-necessary that (1), and if (1) entails that S will occur tomorrow, then it is now-necessary that S will occur tomorrow. (Transfer of Necessity Principle)
(5) Therefore, it is now-necessary that S will occur tomorrow. (2, 3, 4)
(6) So, S is fated. It will occur out of necessity.

All of these arguments can be generalized to any future event that is entailed by past truth, past infallible foreknowledge, or the conjunction of past history and causal laws.[3] I have let the proposition

---

[3] The fact that determinism is the claim that the past + physical laws entail the entire future is compatible with the distinction many philosophers make between logical necessity and physical necessity. It is physically necessary and not logically necessary that the future will be what it will be given the past because the laws of nature do not hold in

S will occur tomorrow stand in for any proposition about any future event. With that assumption, universal fatalism follows.

Notice that the arguments are identical except for the first premise. The form of all three arguments is exactly the same. Using the term nec_T to mean "it is temporally necessary (now-necessary)," and nec_L to mean "it is logically necessary," all the arguments have the following form:

(1) $nec_T\ p$
(2) $nec_L\ (p \to q)$
(3) Therefore, $nec_T\ q$

The underlying principle licensing the inference to (3) mixes two kinds of necessity, but many philosophers find the principle highly plausible because it is the analogue of the most basic axiom of modal logic, Axiom K: $nec_L\ (p \to q) \to [nec_L p \to nec_L q]$, which amounts to the same thing as saying that if it is logically necessary that p, and if it is logically necessary that if p then q, then it is logically necessary that q.

It is interesting that the identity of structure in these arguments has often been overlooked, and they have been treated differently in philosophical history. Generally, not many philosophers have accepted the argument that future truth entails fatalism,[4] but many accept the argument that infallible divine foreknowledge entails fatalism. For centuries there has been controversy over the argument

---

all possible worlds. But the determinist claims that it is logically necessary that if the laws and the past are as they are, the future will be what it will be. The assumption is that the laws of nature are universal and invariable. Some philosophers deny that laws of nature exist in this sense, e.g., Nancy Cartwright (1999), Bas van Fraassen (1989), and John Dupré (2001).

[4] Fischer and Todd's (2015) anthology of papers on foreknowledge and fatalism includes a section on the logic of future contingents, which shows increasing seriousness in the treatment of the idea that future contingents lack truth value, arising from concerns about logical fatalism. David Hunt (2020 note 1) remarks on the change when discussing presentism and fatalism.

that causal determinism entails fatalism, with many philosophers arguing that causal necessitation does not take away free will, while others arguing that it does. But all three arguments arise from the combination of the necessity of the past and the same transfer of necessity principle. That suggests that if one of the arguments is stronger than another, the difference is not deep.

In Part One I will argue in a sequence of steps that combining the necessity of the past with the transfer of necessity is incoherent. I will start with the challenge of theological fatalism, and I will present the strongest argument I know of for the conclusion that infallible divine foreknowledge entails the lack of free will. I will then gradually uncover a more general dilemma that has nothing to do with God, infallibility, or free will. My conclusion in Part One will be that the idea of the necessity of the past as a temporally asymmetrical modality to which a transfer of necessity principle applies is inconsistent with a number of independent metaphysical, scientific, or theological theses that different people believe are highly likely to be true for different reasons. There is a deep incoherence in our thinking about the contrast between past and future. In Part Two I will examine another interpretation of the necessity of the past—the causal closure of the past. That leads to a different set of fatalist arguments and responses and to related problems in the logic of time. In Part Three I will give my conjectures on what remains of the arrow of time.

Part One
The (Incoherent) Root of Traditional Fatalist Arguments

Section 1. Beginning with theological fatalism

1.1. Our primary argument

Fatalist arguments arise from the discovery of a possibly serious consequence of a thesis that is highly plausible within a certain domain of discourse—the thesis that all propositions about the future have a truth value, the thesis of divine infallibility, or the thesis of causal determinism. Historically, the alleged fatalist commitments of these theses have been treated independently. Traditional theists discuss divine foreknowledge and human free will, but that problem has usually been ignored by non-theists. Causal determinism gets attention in the literature on free will but not in other areas of metaphysics. Logical fatalism is often treated as a trivial problem that can be solved by clear-headed attention to the nature of propositions. But the striking similarity in these arguments begs us to look at them together. If there are three arguments with the same structure, there might be others. If one has a problematic feature, so might the others. A solution to one argument might apply to the others, and if it does not, their similarity should alert us that there is more to be said. In this part of the book, I will begin with a version of the argument for theological fatalism that is valid and as clear as I can make it and which has no extraneous premises. I will use this argument to focus on the primary elements that generate the fatalist conclusion. My goal is to see whether there is an underlying problem in all three arguments, and if so, what the rejection of the form of argument in this part tells us about the logic of time.

The most basic element of fatalist arguments is the Principle of the Necessity of the Past, which is informally expressed in the adage, "There is no use crying over spilled milk." That adage is about human power, and I will discuss versions of the fatalist argument formulated directly in terms of human power in Part Two, but my arguments in Part One proceed from the ancient idea of the necessity of the past going back to the oldest known forms of fatalist arguments that we see in Aristotle's Sea Battle Argument in *De Interpretatione* 9 and in the Master Argument of Diodorus Cronus (4th–3rd centuries BCE).

The Master Argument was widely discussed for hundreds of years as a puzzle in modal logic. Diodorus' formulation of the argument has been lost, but according to Epictetus (2008) (*Discourses* ii. 19), the argument attempts to demonstrate the inconsistency of three propositions: (1) Every true proposition about the past is necessary, (2) an impossibility does not follow from a possibility, and (3) there are propositions that are possible but are neither true nor will be true. Diodorus used (1) and (2) to argue for the falsehood of (3). All false propositions are impossible.

The inconsistency in these three propositions is not straightforward, but Diodorus seems to have in mind something like the following: Assume that (3) is true. Some event will happen in the future, but it is now possible that it will not happen. Since it is true that it will happen, it was true in the past that it will happen. But (1) tells us that past truths are necessary, so it is necessary that it will happen and impossible that it will not happen. But (2) tells us that an impossibility does not follow from a possibility, so assumption (3) contradicts (1) and (2). There is no event which is such that it will happen in the future, yet it is possible that it does not happen.

This is a form of the puzzle of logical fatalism, and it utilizes both the principle of the necessity of the past and the logical entailments of modal logic, the key elements of the arguments I will discuss in this part of the book. The Master Argument was a touchstone for debates about fatalism among the Stoic logicians, who connected it with their metaphysics of fate. Since they equated fate with god, with providence, and with the reason that controls the world, that broadened the reach of the argument from a logical puzzle to the problem of theological fatalism, so the Christian dilemma of divine foreknowledge and human free will had a background of many centuries in the pre-Christian era.[1] The foreknowledge dilemma was examined by Augustine (4th–5th centuries), Boethius (6th century), Aquinas (13th century), Ockham (14th century), Suarez and Molina (16th century), and many other philosophers from late antiquity up to the present era. A classic statement of the theological version was given by Aquinas as an objection to God's knowledge of future contingents:

> Furthermore, every conditional proposition of which the antecedent is absolutely necessary must have an absolutely necessary consequent. For the antecedent is to the consequent as principles are to the conclusion: and from necessary principles only a necessary conclusion can follow, as is proved in Poster. i. But this is a true conditional, *If God knew that this thing will be, it will be*, for the knowledge of God is only of true things. Now the antecedent conditional of this is absolutely necessary, because it is eternal and because it is signified as past. Therefore the consequent is also absolutely necessary. Therefore whatever God knows, is necessary; and so the knowledge of God is not of contingent things. (ST I q. 14.a 13 obj. 2)

Notice how easily the argument of Diodorus was transposed into a theological problem. Similar arguments continued to be debated

---

[1] See Bobzien (1998) for an extensive treatment of fate, determinism, and freedom in Stoic philosophy. Bobzien discusses the Stoic identities mentioned above on 45ff.

up to the later 20th century and beyond. Both logical and theological fatalist arguments were formulated as puzzles about necessity, possibility, and contingency, and the necessity of the past was assumed to be a form of necessity in the logical sense. The necessity of the past was given a precise analysis in the 14th century by William of Ockham, and his brilliant examination of what he called necessity *per accidens* became a benchmark for a large contemporary literature beginning in the 1970s and 1980s, stimulated by a paper by Marilyn Adams (1967). The Ockhamist idea of the necessity of the past plays an important role in all the arguments I will discuss in Part One. In recent decades an alternative interpretation of the necessity of the past that divorces it from modal logic has become popular. That will be the topic of Part Two.

I have begun by calling the Ockhamist idea of the necessity of the past "now-necessity." It is a temporally relative necessity, a kind of necessity that a proposition has now but not when it was about something still future. Ockham called the necessity of the past necessity *per accidens*, or accidental necessity. What makes it accidental in his view is that it is a necessity that a proposition acquires at a certain moment of time, the time that the event it expresses occurs.[2] Before the event, the proposition expressing it is true but not necessary. Once the event occurs, the proposition is both true and necessary. Accidental necessity licenses inferences like those we would draw from other forms of necessity, although I do not believe Ockham explicitly referred to the transfer of necessity principle that we will use in our primary argument below.

Accidental necessity is the idea that time has a modal arrow. Time is linear and directional. As time moves forward, what was first contingent becomes necessary. There are other arrows of time that will come up in this book. For instance, the directionality of

---

[2] Of course, Ockham was aware that not every proposition expresses an event that occurs at a particular moment of time, but the propositions we are concerned with are of that kind.

time underlies the fact that we remember the past, not the future. We deliberate about the future, not the past. We cause events in the future, not the past. We experience time as flowing inexorably from past to future. We also know that there is a temporal asymmetry of entropy, which means that time moves in the direction of greater disorder in an isolated system. These commonsense and observational assumptions about time do not square well with the temporal symmetries of physics, and the issue of what time is, is as vexing to physicists as to philosophers, but modern physics has not succeeded in shaking most of our notions about the linearity and directionality of time. We will return to these assumptions in the conclusion of this book.

The idea of the necessity of the past will come up repeatedly, but one confusion should be eliminated at the start. The necessity of the past is not the idea that we cannot *change* the past. If there is only one timeline of events, it is trivially true that we cannot change what did happen into what didn't happen, or what didn't happen into what did happen. That would mean that there is one past "before" the change and another past "after" the change, and I assume that that is incoherent.[3] For the same reason, we cannot change the future if there is a single timeline going from past to future. We cannot change what *will* happen into what will not happen or what will not happen into what will happen. Change is not the issue. The issue is the nature of necessity as it applies to time.

To review, the Transfer of Accidental Necessity Principle is the following:

$[\text{nec}_T\, p \text{ and nec}_L\, (p \to q)] \to \text{nec}_T\, q.$

In English: If p is accidentally necessary (now-necessary) and p entails q, then q is accidentally necessary.

---

[3] Some time travel movies such as *Back to the Future* (1985) seem to me to be incoherent for this reason, whereas others such as *Interstellar* (2014) make sense.

In addition, our argument will use the Principle of Alternate Possibilities, which says that if a person S cannot refrain from doing A when she does A, S does not do A freely.

What I have said so far should be enough to state the core argument of Part One of this book.

Argument for theological fatalism

(1) Suppose God infallibly believed yesterday that S will do A tomorrow.

From the principle of the necessity of the past we get

(2) It is now-necessary that God believed yesterday that S will do A tomorrow.

From the definition of divine infallibility we get

(3) Necessarily, if God believed yesterday that S will do A tomorrow, then S will do A tomorrow.

Following Ockham, it follows from (2), (3), and the Transfer of Accidental Necessity Principle that

(4) It is now-necessary that S will do A tomorrow.

It follows from the idea that accidental necessity is a form of necessity that

(5) If it is now-necessary that S will do A tomorrow, then S cannot refrain from doing A tomorrow.

The Principle of Alternate Possibilities states that

(6) If S cannot refrain from doing A tomorrow, then S does not do A tomorrow freely.

By (4), (5), (6), and hypothetical syllogism we can conclude

(7) S does not do A tomorrow freely.

If, as traditional theists believe, God is omniscient as well as infallible, this argument can be generalized to any act in the future. Universal fatalism appears to follow.

There are many variations of this argument in the literature on theological fatalism, but I do not believe that any of the variations deviates from this version in any significant way. In any case, I think that this version is among the best, and I will highlight features of the argument that are common to all fatalist arguments based on the necessity of the past.

Sometimes people discuss invalid forms of the argument for theological fatalism that we will need to dismiss. I have heard people argue as follows: The definition of "knowledge" analytically includes the truth of the proposition known. The sentence "S knows p" entails "p is true." That means that if theological fatalism is a problem, it would be a problem for anybody's knowledge of the future. But we do not worry about that, so why worry when the knower is God? The theological fatalist argument is a sham.

This move interprets the fatalist argument as fallaciously claiming that the simple fact of knowing the proposition p entails fatalism because knowing p entails that p is true, and if p is in the future, fatalism follows. Notice that this interpretation attempts to reduce theological fatalism to logical fatalism. The problem is just the truth of p when p is future.

Unfortunately, whatever we think of logical fatalism, which I will address later, theological fatalism cannot be dismissed so easily. The problem is not that God knows the future, a state that you and I can have, but that God knows the future infallibly. God's infallible beliefs about the future are needed to generate the problem. To see why, consider the way the fatalist argument would have to proceed if the issue was the same as ordinary human knowing:

(1) Sam knew p_{fut} in the past (Assumption)
(2) It is now-necessary that Sam knew p_{fut} in the past (Necessity of the past)
(3) (1) entails that p_{fut} is true. (Definition of "true")
(4) If (2) and (3), then it is now-necessary that p_{fut} is true. (Transfer of Accidental Necessity)
(5) So, it is now-necessary that p_{fut} is true.

But premise (2) is false. It is not now-necessary that Sam knew that something in the future would occur because it is not now-necessary that Sam was in a state of knowledge rather than justified (or epistemically virtuous or warranted) belief unless Sam is infallible. Consider something an ordinary person like Sam could know about the future, something that is not necessitated for other reasons, and therefore, something he could not know infallibly. It could be an event that is almost surely going to happen, perhaps a holiday that will give Sam a day off from work. Let us suppose that it is true that Sam will get a day off in one month, and Sam has good reason to believe it, good enough that we say his belief state satisfies the conditions for knowledge given that his belief is true. Sam does indeed know that he will get the day off. But ordinary knowing does not preclude the possibility of being mistaken. If it did, we humans would have very little knowledge. Sam knows that he will get the day off, given the ordinary meaning of "knows," but the state he is in does not rule out the possibility that the holiday will be canceled for some reason, which means that it is possible that Sam's past state is only a state of belief, not knowledge. Premise (2) above is false. It is not now-necessary that he knew that he would get the holiday because it is not now-necessary that he believed the truth. Therefore, we cannot conclude (4).

What this example shows is that the problem of theological fatalism requires the infallibility of God's past belief state, not simply that it was a state of knowledge. The example also shows that it does not matter whether we frame the problem in terms of infallible divine belief or infallible divine knowledge. Infallibility is the operative feature.

There is another fallacious form of the fatalist argument, one that uses an invalid inference and therefore must be rejected. Suppose we skip the premise that says that God's past infallible knowledge is now-necessary. The argument would become:

(1) God infallibly believed that p_{fut}.
(2) Nec (If (1) then p_{fut}).
(3) Therefore, Nec p_{fut}.

This argument has the following invalid form:

(1) p
(2) Nec (p →q)
(3) Therefore, Nec q

To see the invalidity, take this example:

(1) Polly lives in California.
(2) Necessarily, if Polly lives in California, Polly lives in the U.S.
(3) Therefore, it is necessary that Polly lives in the U.S.

Presumably, there is no necessity for Polly to live in California, and therefore there is no necessity that she lives in the U.S.

This mistake shows that the validity of the fatalist argument above requires the premise of the necessity of the past. The falsity of premise (2) in the argument about ordinary human knowledge shows that the fatalist argument requires the premise about divine infallibility. So, the argument for theological fatalism requires both the assumption that God had infallible beliefs about the future and the premise that the past is "necessary" in a sense that is transferred to the future via a transfer of necessity principle. These two premises are crucial.

The theological premise in our argument for theological fatalism will be accepted or rejected for reasons that are independent of the topic of this book, but before proceeding, I want to look more closely at the idea of the necessity of the past since it is critical for all the fatalist arguments of Part One.

1.2. The Ockhamist idea of accidental necessity

Ockham grounded his idea of accidental necessity in the act/potency distinction, a metaphysical conception of time and change inherited from Aristotle.[4] To speak of potency is his way of recognizing that there is more than one way the world can go. There is potency for both *p* and *not p* when what is actual has not yet determined which way potency will be reduced to act. The clearest and most philosophically satisfying way to interpret Ockham is that there are three ways the potency for *not p* can be lost. It can be lost because

(a) causes sufficient to make *p* true have already occurred, or
(b) the event that proposition *p* is about occurs, or
(c) *p* is metaphysically necessary, so there never was any potency for *not p*.

---

[4] The distinction between potency (or potentiality) and act (or actuality) was important for Aristotle's explanation of motion and change, and it appears throughout his works, especially in *Metaphysics* Bk IX and in *Physics* Bk III. He defines motion as follows: "The fulfillment of what exists potentially, in so far as it exists potentially, is motion" (*Physics* 201a 10). Aristotle's distinction between potency and act was one of the most important philosophical discoveries in ancient history.

Case (a) is one in which *p* is causally necessary. Case (b) is one in which *p* is accidentally necessary. Case (c) is one in which *p* is metaphysically necessary. These are all forms of the necessity of *p* according to Ockham, and all are connected with the lack of potency for *not p*. The reduction from potency to act is what makes an event move from contingent to necessary, and the proposition expressing it to move from contingent to necessary.

It is important that the temporal modality Ockham calls accidental necessity or contingency is not confused with causal modalities. A proposition *p* can be accidentally necessary but causally contingent, and it can be causally necessary but accidentally contingent. Presumably *the sun will rise tomorrow* is causally necessary even though it is accidentally contingent, whereas *I dropped a pile of books yesterday* might be a causally contingent truth even though it is accidentally necessary. If *p* is necessary in either sense, there is no potency for *not p*, but for different reasons. The same point applies to metaphysical necessity. *God exists* could be metaphysically necessary, and so there is no potency in things for God's nonexistence, but not because causes sufficient for God's existence have occurred, and not because the proposition that God exists is about something that happened in the past. A proposition *p* is necessary when there is no potency for *not p* for any of these three reasons.[5] So, a proposition that is causally contingent can be necessary for reasons that do not pertain to causes, and a proposition that is accidentally contingent can be necessary for reasons of causation, not temporal order. That means that a proposition *p* that is accidentally contingent might not be contingent full stop. It might be causally necessary. If *p* is causally necessary, there is no

---

[5] This is an example in which I think Ockham confuses matters. He proposes that *God exists* does not have the necessity of the past because the proposition *God existed in the past* entails the proposition *God will exist in the future*. Perhaps so, but it should be clear that both *God existed in the past* and *God will exist in the future* are metaphysically necessary. The idea that the proposition *God exists* does not have the necessity of the past was discussed by Marilyn Adams (1967) in the paper that brought Ockham's solution to the dilemma of divine foreknowledge into the contemporary literature.

longer potency for not *p*, but not because of the movement of time. Although I do not find this interpretation of accidental necessity explicitly stated in Ockham, it seems to me that it is the best interpretation because it avoids confusion about the different grounds for the necessity or contingency of propositions.

It is important for Ockham's account of accidental necessity that truth and necessity are distinct. According to Marilyn Adams' construction of Ockham's position (Ockham 1983), he accepts the following thesis:

(T1) x's being A at t_m is determinate at t_n if and only if *at some time or other* there is (was, will be) no potency in things for x's not being (having been, going to be) A at t_m. (10)

Adams says that this allows a thing future relative to t_n to be determinate at t_n even if nothing real or actual in the past or present relative to t_n necessitates its future existence. What is required is that something that exists at some time or other settles its future existence (10).

Ockham also affirms the thesis that propositions are determinately true or determinately false by corresponding or failing to correspond to what is determinately actual at some time. So, Ockham endorses the following thesis about truth:

(T2) *x is (was, will be)* A *at* t_m is determinately true at t_n if and only if at some time or other there is (was, will be) no potency in things for x's not being (having been, being going to be) A at t_m. (10)

That means that *p* can be determinately true at time *t* even though it is accidentally contingent at *t*. This interpretation of the relation between truth and necessity permits Ockham to escape logical fatalism in his handling of Aristotle's famous Sea Battle Argument, which I will discuss presently.

Adams makes another point about Ockham that is important for fatalist arguments. She observes that Ockham is talking about real modalities, not logical modalities (5). That is significant because it affects the way we think of the connection between accidental necessity and principles of modal logic. Ockham's modalities all derive from the basic Aristotelian idea of potency and act, which is a metaphysical distinction. Necessity is what is settled by what is now in act. The contingent is what is now in potency. It is something that has not been settled by what is now in act. Propositions are true when they coincide with what is in act at some time or other.

We might wonder why Ockham thought of the idea of accidental necessity. His assumption is that there is much in the future that is contingent. For many propositions *p*, there is now potency for *p* and potency for *not p*. Neither metaphysical principles nor the sequence of causes has determined *p*, nor has it determined *not p*. Accidental necessity is something that an event/proposition acquires because of the passage of time. There would be no reason to talk about accidental necessity at all if everything in the future was already necessary because it is causally necessary. The act/potency distinction would be irrelevant if there are no propositions *p* such that there exists both the potency for *p* and the potency for *not p* at a given time. Accidental necessity should not be a redundant form of necessity in a world in which the existence of all contrary potencies has already been eliminated by the causal structure of the world or some metaphysical thesis.

Recognizing that Ockham's modalities are real features of the world, we can give a simple way to understand what he means by necessity:

It is necessary that *p* = there is no potency for *not p*.

It is contingent that *p* = there is potency for *p* and potency for *not p*.

The fact that the event expressed by *p* occurs *now* is one of the reasons why there is no potency for *not p* from now on, but, as we have seen, it is not the only way *p* can be necessary.

I will return to this pair of definitions in subsequent fatalist arguments. Sometimes I will follow Ockham in using Aristotle's terminology, but I think that we need not be Aristotelians to recognize that this pair of definitions expresses deep intuitions that most of us have about the difference between what is and what might be. The act/potency distinction is also a way to explain change from what might be to what is. I surmise that even though it is not common for contemporary philosophers to speak in terms of act and potency, we do in fact speak of the difference between what is and what might be, and the change from what might be to what is. The difference between what is and what might be is grounded in reality, the way the world is constructed. That is what the act/potency distinction attempts to capture.

It is important that accidental necessity is literally a kind of necessity according to Ockham and his contemporary followers. That means that necessary propositions have a number of logical transformations:

It is necessary that *p* = It is not possible that *not p*
It is necessary that *not p* = It is not possible that *p*
It is contingent that *p* = It is possible that *p* and it is possible that *not p*

As applied to accidental necessity, we get:

It is accidentally necessary that *p* = It is not accidentally possible that *not p*
It is accidentally necessary that *not p* = It is not accidentally possible that *p*

It is accidentally contingent that p = It is accidentally possible that p and it is accidentally possible that *not p*.

The idea that the necessity of the past is literally a form of necessity gives those philosophers discussing fatalism a powerful logical tool, and it immediately leads to the use of the other premise crucial to the fatalist conclusion—the Transfer of Accidental Necessity Principle. Although this principle can be criticized because it mixes two senses of necessity, it is significant that the principle is based on an axiom intended to express what necessity *means*. If some form of necessity does not satisfy it, we would be justified in concluding that it is not a form of necessity at all.

Section 2. Unraveling theological fatalism

2.1. First stage: Is the problem uniquely about God's infallibility and fatalism? No.

Notice that there is nothing in our argument for theological fatalism that refers to the personhood of God or to the attributes of God other than infallible foreknowledge. The argument is clearly intended to demonstrate an incompatibility between infallible foreknowledge by any being whatever and human free will. Of course, God is the prime candidate for an actual infallible believer, but a focus on God hides the deeper fact that if there is free will in the world—in fact, if there are any contingent events in nature, the argument purports to show that it is metaphysically impossible that anybody is infallible or becomes infallible in their knowledge about free acts or those events.[6] But the alleged connection between the ability to act freely and the epistemic ability of a completely independent being is exceedingly strange. Surely there is a prima facie

---

[6] David Hunt (1998) showed many years ago that the theological problem and the metaphysical problem of infallible foreknowledge are distinct.

principle that knowing *p* does not affect the truth of *p*. In fact, it is almost always thought to be the reverse. The truth of *p* comes first in logical order; knowing *p* is derivative. Of course, the adherent of the incompatibility of infallibility and free will does not deny this principle in general. It is only in the special case in which knowing is infallible that the principle does not hold. This is a problem for anybody, not just theists. It is a metaphysical problem. How can a mind's power of grasping reality affect the reality that is known? Granted, we know from the observer effect in quantum physics that the process of observation disturbs what is observed, but that puzzle is not about a special power of knowing that makes it impossible that what is known is otherwise. Using Aristotelian terminology, how can a mind's ability to know make it the case that there is no potency in things? Even more odd, suppose a being who was first always correct but not infallible then becomes infallible. Do all future contingent events suddenly become necessary? There seems to be a bizarre relationship between knowledge and what it is knowledge *of*.

Let us look at the generalized argument for the incompatibility of infallible foreknowledge and human free will. The argument is the same as our primary argument for theological fatalism, only it postulates a possible infallible foreknower that is neutral on the being's other attributes.

Argument that infallible believing entails fatalism
Consider the possibility of a being whose beliefs about future human choices are infallible. Let us call that being IB.

(1) IB infallibly believed yesterday that S will do A tomorrow. (Assumption)
(2) It is now-necessary that (1). (Necessity of the Past)
(3) Necessarily, if IB believed yesterday that S will do A tomorrow, then S will do A tomorrow. (Definition of "infallibility.")

(4) It is now-necessary that S will do A tomorrow. (2, 3, Transfer of Necessity)
(5) If (4), then S cannot refrain from doing A tomorrow (Definition of "necessity.")
(6) If S cannot refrain from doing A tomorrow, S will not do A tomorrow freely (Principle of Alternate Possibilities)
(7) Therefore, S will not do A tomorrow freely. (4, 5, 6 hypothetical syllogism)

This argument shows an apparent inconsistency between free will and infallible believing by any being whatsoever. Identifying that being with God is not necessary for the argument.

The fatalist argument is almost always treated as a dilemma. Either we do not have free will or there is no infallible foreknower. Writers who want to affirm both free will and infallible foreknowledge therefore need to find a false premise or an invalid inference in the argument. I have chosen to present only valid arguments so that we can see what would have to be denied by someone who wants to affirm the first premise but also wants to escape the fatalist conclusion. Most putative "solutions" to the problem of theological fatalism point to a feature of God that hopefully escapes the unwanted commitment to fatalism. It is possible that some of these solutions succeed, but even if they do, they do not address the more general argument above. Either there is a solution to the general dilemma of infallible foreknowledge or there is not. If there is, the solution would presumably apply to the dilemma of theological fatalism, and it would not be necessary to give a special theological solution. If there is not, that would mean that there is a problem with the assumption that there is an infallible foreknower that is escaped only in the special case of divine foreknowledge. That might satisfy some theists, but the problem in the general argument still needs to be addressed. The fact that the dilemma of divine infallible foreknowledge and human free will can be so easily generalized shows that the problem goes beyond its theological interest.

Proposed solutions to the dilemma of infallible foreknowledge and human free will that are effective only against the theological form of the problem are therefore limited in their effectiveness against the possibility of fatalism in spite of their theological relevance. I can think of four such solutions.

The first is the position that God is timeless. This solution goes back to Boethius and was adopted by Aquinas.[7] It has many contemporary defenders, particularly those who favor Thomistic theology. This solution proposes that if God exists outside of time, his belief states are outside of time, and there is no worry that his belief states have the necessity of the past. The first premise of the argument for theological fatalism is false because God does not believe anything in the past, nor does God believe anything in the present or in the future. God is omniscient and infallible, but he believes everything timelessly. Elsewhere I have argued that this solution is inadequate (Zagzebski 2011),[8] but my point here is that even if the solution works as a response to divine foreknowledge, it has no bearing on the general argument for the incompatibility of infallible foreknowledge and human free will.

A second solution that is explicitly theistic is William P. Alston's (1986) position that God does not have belief states. Alston adopts the common position that believing is a propositional attitude; it is a mental state directed at propositions. But God's mental states are not like ours, directed at discrete propositions. God grasps all concrete wholes at once, without needing to divide them into separate propositional bits. Even if God did assent to propositions, Alston argues, since God grasps all of reality at once, propositions are superfluous. This approach is Thomistic in spirit, and it refers to the distinctive way a divine being knows, a way that would not apply to

---

[7] Boethius (1962), Bk V Prose 6. Aquinas ST I-I, q. 14.a 13, reply obj. 3.
[8] In that paper I argue, among other things, that the timelessness solution works only if the timeless realm is not outside our control. But if there is a Principle of the Necessity of Eternity parallel to the Principle of the Necessity of the Past, another version of the fatalist argument can be formulated.

the general problem of an infallible but non-divine being, one who presumably believes propositions.

A third solution that is explicitly theistic is Molinism, the theory that God knows the entire contingent future by combining his knowledge of his creative will with his knowledge of so-called counterfactuals of freedom, true propositions expressing what a given free creature would freely choose in any possible circumstance. Such knowledge is called "Middle Knowledge."[9] By knowing each future circumstance and what a free creature would freely choose in that circumstance, God can know all future human acts infallibly without jeopardizing the freedom of his creatures. Notice that this solution gets its force from a theory about the power of God to know truths beyond the reach of any non-divine being. The approach will not be successful against the general dilemma of infallible but non-divine foreknowledge and human free will unless any imagined infallible being has other powers of God.

There is another problem with the Molinist solution that makes it unclear how it can even escape the theological form of the argument. Which premise is being denied by the Molinist? Molinism is attractive because it offers an account of how God's foreknowledge operates, but it does not offer an objection to any premise of the fatalist argument. The Molinist solution needs another move to avoid the conclusion.[10] However, my interest here is not in objecting to Molinism but in showing its inability to address the alleged fatalist consequences of infallible but non-divine believing.

---

[9] The doctrine of Middle Knowledge was vehemently debated in the 16th century, with the version of Luis de Molina, referred to as "Molinism," getting the most attention in the contemporary literature. It has received strong support by Thomas Flint (1998) and Eef Dekker (2000).

[10] For this reason, some philosophers, such as John Martin Fischer (2011b) and William Hasker (1989, 18) say that Molinism should not be called a solution to theological fatalism. In his introduction to Molina (1988), Alfred Freddoso argues that Molina rejects the transfer of accidental necessity under entailment (63–66). That move directly attacks the fatalist argument. Thomas Flint (1998) appears to accept some form of Ockhamism in addition to defending Middle Knowledge.

What about the Ockhamist solution? Ockham's idea is that even if God is in time, God's beliefs lack the necessity of the past because every such state is not strictly in the past. It is in the "soft past," in the same category as the fact that it was true yesterday that S would do A tomorrow. The fact that a proposition about the future was true yesterday is a fact that is partly about the past and partly about the future. Similarly, Ockham argues, propositions about God's past beliefs (and God's past existence) are not strictly about the past. Like past truths about the future, they are in the soft past because they entail facts about the future. This approach is theistic, but it has an advantage over the other approaches I have mentioned since it does not refer to a divine property other than infallibility to escape the premise about the necessity of God's past beliefs. Presumably, Ockham could say (if he thought of it) that the past beliefs of *any* infallible believer are soft facts. If that could be made to work, the Ockhamist would have a solution to the general problem of infallible foreknowledge as well as to the theological problem.

The same cannot be said for the solution I called "Thomistic Ockhamism" in my first foreknowledge book (1991, Chapter 3). There I proposed strengthening Ockham's idea that God's beliefs are soft facts in time by adding Aquinas's idea that God knows everything all at once, a point that was also taken by Alston in his solution. If God's knowing is not divided into discrete bits occurring at particular moments of time, then even if God had beliefs in the past, he had those beliefs in a way that does not separate his past knowing from his future knowing. God's knowing state spreads out over time, and it is no more in the past than in the future. God's single all-encompassing knowing state therefore does not have the necessity of the past. But as much as I like this solution, it has the same problem as the other solutions that use Thomas' account of the divine nature. It is not applicable to the problem of infallible believing by a non-divine being.

The Newcomb puzzle is revealing because it recognizes that there is a deeper form of the fatalist problem that is not theological and which highlights the two basic assumptions—the necessity of the past, and the assumption of infallible, or alternatively, always accurate beliefs about the future.[11] In the puzzle, we imagine a game show where the host has amazing abilities, but she is not God. The game host puts two boxes on the stage, and she puts $1,000 in Box A. She does not tell you what she put in Box B. She says that you can choose either the contents of Box B or the contents of both Box A and Box B. She has made a prediction about what you will choose, and she has never been wrong in the many years the game has been played. If she predicted that you would choose just Box B, she put $1 million in Box B. If she predicted that you would choose both boxes, she put nothing in Box B. The question is, what do you do?

Here is the argument for choosing only one box. If the game host is always right, then if you choose one box, she would have predicted that you would choose one box and she would have put $1 million in that box. If you choose two boxes, she would have predicted that you would choose both boxes, and she would have put nothing in Box B. So you would only get $1,000. You should choose one box.

Here is the argument for choosing both boxes. The game host has already made her prediction, and she has already put either $1 million or nothing in Box B. Nothing is going to change what she put in that box. If she has put $1 million in the box, you might as well choose both boxes because then you will get an extra $1,000. On the other hand, if she has put nothing in Box B, then again you should choose both boxes because at least you get $1,000 instead of nothing. Either way, you come out $1,000 ahead.

The one-box advocate focuses on the game host's predictive power. If we can imagine that the game host is infallible, the game

---

[11] This puzzle was originally proposed by William Newcomb but never published. It became well-known after its first publication by Robert Nozick (1969).

host is like IB in the argument above. Her infallibility means that there is no possibility that there is not a 100 percent correlation between choosing one box and getting the million dollars. Suppose, however, that she is not infallible but has never been wrong. In that case, it is possible that she is wrong, and the decision to choose one box is not as obvious, but it might still be rational to assume that her prediction is correct. Either way, trust in the game host's ability is the deciding factor for choosing one box. In contrast, the two-boxer focuses on the necessity of the past. It has already been done and cannot be undone. The argument between the one-boxer and the two-boxer, then, reveals the conflict between the fact that the game host is infallible (or never wrong) and the necessity of the past.[12]

What is particularly interesting to me about this puzzle is that there is no commonly accepted solution to it, and both choices seem equally rational. That should alert us that there might be something wrong in the way the puzzle is set up, and if so, there might be something wrong in the way the fatalist argument is set up. The coherence problem in the Newcomb case is even worse if we alter the story in ways that seem realistic. For instance, suppose Box B becomes torn and you can see what is inside. Surely, that would affect your choice. But what would it reveal? If the story is coherent, it should reveal to you the choice you will make before you make it. If there is nothing in the box, that means you will choose both boxes. If there is a million dollars in the box, that means you will choose only Box B. But which is cause and which is effect? Does seeing the $1 million in the box cause you to choose one box? If it does, and if the game host's prediction is caused by your choice, it looks like there is a causal loop:

---

[12] It is interesting that whereas some philosophers advocate taking one box whether the predictor is infallible or just inerrant, John Martin Fischer (1994, 106) is a one-boxer if the predictor is infallible and a two-boxer if the predictor is inerrant but not infallible.

The predictor puts $1 million in the box.
That causes you to see $1 million in the box when you look inside.
That causes you to choose one box.
That causes the predictor to predict you will choose one box.
That causes the predictor to put $1 million in the box.

Even if causal loops are not obviously incoherent, they are mystifying. The Newcomb problem should lead us to wonder if there is an underlying contradiction between infallibility and the necessity of the past. If there is, we will need an explanation of the root of the contradiction and its implications.

The Calvinist doctrine of predestination can be formulated like the Newcomb puzzle.[13] Suppose that God predestines you to be saved if he infallibly predicts that you will accept grace, whereas he predestines you to be condemned if he infallibly predicts that you will refuse grace. Let us also imagine that accepting grace means that you live a good life, whereas refusing grace means that you live a morally bad life. That puts you in the same situation as the Newcomb game. We may assume that God made the decision to save you or condemn you before you were born. But now, how should you choose to live? If you are like the one-boxer, you will reason that you should live a good life because that will mean that it was predestined that you would be saved. If you are like the two-boxer, you will reason that if God predestined you to be saved, it is already done. You might as well go ahead and do what you want rather than to live a morally good life (assuming that they are not the same thing). If God predestined you to be damned, then again, you might as well go ahead and do what you want since at least you would get to do what you want before you are damned. The predestination puzzle also has the problem of distinguishing cause from

---

[13] Howard Sobel (1998) and John Martin Fischer (1994, 106–107) interpret the doctrine of predestination as a Newcomb puzzle.

effect. Does God's predestination cause you to choose to live a good life, or does your choice to live a good life cause God to predestine you to be saved, or is there a causal circle?

The theology of predestination is not necessarily a Newcomb problem, but I have described a version that is. It is significant that a theological Newcomb puzzle raises metaphysical issues that are not simply relevant to an in-house discussion of theology. The relationship between the power of infallible knowing and the modal status of the past is extremely vexing.

The moral of the first stage of my argument reducing theological fatalism to a deeper problem is this: The dilemma of divine foreknowledge and human freedom is easily generalizable to a problem that is not uniquely theological but is metaphysical. That should bother the non-theist as much as the theist because it purports to show a logical incompatibility between the existence of human freedom, the conditions for which are presumably metaphysical, and an epistemic power of some independent being. That seems to force us into a very odd view of the world, one that conflicts with the intuitively plausible principle that the truth of p comes first in logical order; knowing p comes second. The structure of the theological fatalist argument shows that the problem is not uniquely about God.

2.2. Second stage: Is the problem uniquely about infallibility and fatalism? No.

The argument of the last section can be generalized further in a way that has nothing to do with free will. As we have seen, Ockham assumed that the past and future are modally contrastive in that there is a kind of necessity that the past has simply in virtue of being past, whereas the future is contingent with respect to that kind of necessity, and that is why propositions about particular events in time acquire this type of necessity only at the time of the event. The past is accidentally necessary, whereas the future is accidentally contingent. As we will see in Part Two, contemporary philosophers have proposed alternative interpretations of the necessity of the past in terms of the lack of causal control rather than necessity, but I am beginning with the idea in its purest logical form, using William of Ockham's account of necessity *per accidens* as a form of necessity rather than inalterability or lack of causal control. On Ockham's account, accidental necessity and contingency attach to a proposition in virtue of the passage of time. The future is contingent *per accidens*; the past is necessary *per accidens*. That is not to deny that the future can have some other kind of necessity, such as causal necessity, nor is it to deny that the past can have some other kind of contingency, such as causal contingency. But since Ockham believed that some events are in potency, he accepted the idea that there are propositions *p* such that there is potency in things for *p* and there is potency in things for *not p* at a given time. Propositions about the future are not all causally necessary. If they were, the idea of accidental necessity loses its point.

The modal difference between past and future defended by Ockham and corresponding to the metaphysical distinction between act and potency is inconsistent with the existence of an infallible foreknower apart from any considerations about free will. The fatalist arguments we have just looked at hide a deeper dilemma that is not about fatalism but about time. That is because of the Ockhamist idea that the passage of time moves the accidentally contingent to the accidentally necessary as the occurrence of events in the future occur. The principle of the necessity of the past has a correlate in the principle of the contingency of the future. The past *qua* past is accidentally necessary; the future *qua* future is accidentally contingent. When we make this difference between accidental necessity and contingency explicit, we can see that it is inconsistent with infallible foreknowledge before we get to a premise about free will.

Argument that infallible believing is inconsistent with accidental necessity/contingency

(1) Suppose that there is (and was before now) an infallible believer IB who has an infallible belief regarding F, a proposition about some future event F.

It follows that

(2) Either IB believed F before now or IB believed *not F* before now.

From (2), the Principle of the Necessity of the Past, and constructive dilemma, we get:

(3) Either it is now-necessary that IB believed F before now or it is now-necessary that IB believed *not F* before now.

From (1) and the definition of infallibility it follows that

(4) Necessarily (IB believed F before now → F is true), and necessarily (IB believed *not F* before now → *not F* is true).

From (3), (4), the Transfer of Accidental Necessity Principle and constructive dilemma we get:

(5) Either it is now-necessary that F is true or it is now-necessary that *not F* is true.

(5) is logically equivalent to

(6) Either it is not now-possible that F is true or it is not now-possible that *not F* is true.

From the Principle of the accidental contingency of the future it follows that

(7) It is now-possible that F is true and it is now-possible that *not F* is true.

But (7) contradicts (5).[14]

From this argument we can see that the contrast between accidental necessity and accidental contingency is inconsistent with infallible foreknowledge. Fatalism makes no appearance in this argument. It is an argument about the logic of time. The argument also reveals an interesting problem in the fatalist use of the idea of the necessity of the past. The fatalist assumes one half of the modal arrow of time in order to argue that there is no arrow. Is there an arrow or not? The fatalist assumes the arrow at the beginning of the argument and then uses the premise of infallible foreknowledge to deny the arrow. That shows at least confusion, and possibly inconsistency, in what is being assumed about the arrow of time in the formulation of the argument.

Here is a possible interpretation of the fatalist use of the arrow of time that is not confused. The fatalist could offer the argument as a *reductio ad absurdum*. The argument would have the following form:

Premise: There is an arrow of time.

From that premise and the intervening steps, the argument leads to the subconclusion:

There is no arrow of time.

---

[14] I first proposed an argument like this in the Appendix to my 1991 foreknowledge book. I repeated it in other papers, including my *Stanford Encyclopedia of Philosophy* entry, "Foreknowledge and Free Will" (2017).

If follows by conjunction that:

There is an arrow of time and there is no arrow of time.

We have derived a contradiction. Therefore, there is no arrow of time. The first premise is false.

I do not know of anybody who converts the fatalist argument into a *reductio*. If the fatalist intends to do so, it should be explicit. If it is not a *reductio*, the implied contradiction between the premise that the necessity of the past is one side of the arrow of time and the conclusion of the argument needs to be addressed.

I have interpreted accidental necessity and contingency as a modality that attaches to the passage of time. All of the past is necessary in this sense and all of the future is contingent in this sense. I believe that that is the clearest and most reasonable interpretation of the modal arrow of time. But there is an alternative interpretation of accidental necessity and contingency that some readers might prefer. Suppose that accidental necessity and contingency apply only to those propositions that are not metaphysically or causally necessary. With that interpretation, the principle of the contingency of the future used in the above argument would require the proviso that proposition F is about an event in the future that is neither metaphysically nor causally necessary. If causal determinism is true, there are no such propositions, and accidental necessity/contingency is irrelevant to the actual world. If causal determinism is false, the argument stands with the modification that F is not causally necessary. Infallible believing is inconsistent with the modality of accidental necessity and contingency on either interpretation of the scope of the accidentally contingent.

Fatalism is important because we care about having free will, and solutions to fatalist arguments that focus on the requirements of free will have warranted an enormous amount of philosophical energy. But my reaction to these ways of avoiding fatalism is the same as my reaction to the distinctively theistic solutions to theological fatalism. Maybe these moves work, and maybe they don't. But if there is a deeper problem that has nothing to do with free will, perhaps it is not necessary for us to work so hard at finding a mistake in the premise about free will, just as it may not be necessary for us to work so hard to find a way around fatalism that focuses on the attributes of God. The underlying problem is not distinctively about God, nor is it distinctively about free will.

The argument I have given here shows an inconsistency in the combination of Ockham's idea of accidental necessity/contingency and the possibility of an infallible believer. That problem cannot be solved by another important response to the standard dilemma of theological fatalism, as well as the parallel problem of causal fatalism: the denial of the Principle of Alternate Possibilities (PAP). That is the principle that free will requires the ability to do otherwise. PAP has many variations, but the particular form of the principle is irrelevant to the argument above since that argument makes no reference to free will.

Fatalism has always been advertised as a clash between some well-known thesis like divine foreknowledge or causal determinism and free will. Much effort has been placed on analyzing free will as a possible way to retain both infallible foreknowledge and free will or causal determinism and free will. My argument here is that the problem arises with the notion of temporally asymmetrical necessity/contingency when combined with a transfer of necessity principle. Something has gone wrong in the argument before we get to the conditions for free will.

Notice also the implications for Open Theism. Open Theists believe that the theological fatalist argument like our primary argument succeeds in showing that divine foreknowledge is incompatible with human free will, and they maintain that God forgoes infallible foreknowledge in order to preserve human freedom. But the argument in this section shows that if past and future are modally contrastive, it is impossible for God or anybody else to have infallible foreknowledge apart from any desire to have free creatures.

Infallible foreknowledge is ruled out by the alleged modal asymmetry of time and the movement from potency to act when an event occurs. God would have to prevent anybody from being infallible if he wanted past and future to be contrasted in the Ockhamist fashion. God's decision about how time is structured is the issue, not free will.

This leads to an interesting question. If God could not create an infallible being in a world in which time is modally asymmetrical, it would be impossible for the incarnate Christ to be infallible. There are, of course, different positions about the mind of Christ and his knowing power, but the argument of this section leads to the conclusion that it would be metaphysically impossible for Jesus Christ to be incarnated with an infallible mind.[15] If God created time with an asymmetrical structure between past and future, he thereby made it impossible for anybody to be infallible.

There are remarkable metaphysical and theological ramifications of unraveling theological fatalism. When we think we have solved one problem, we find another. It is very tempting to focus on a particular argument that we hope is unsound, and then congratulate ourselves when we think we have found a problem in it, but all too often, another problem lurks around the corner. A philosopher's job is never done.

2.3. Third stage: Is the problem uniquely about infallibility and time? No.

The problem in the logic of time is even deeper than a problem about combining infallibility with accidental necessity. When we looked carefully at the argument for theological fatalism in section

---

[15] I point out in Zagzebski (2011) that those who accept the timelessness solution because they believe temporal infallibility leads to fatalism must accept the impossibility that Jesus Christ had infallible foreknowledge.

2.1, we noticed that the argument does not rely upon any properties of God except infallible foreknowledge. When we looked at the argument that infallible foreknowledge is inconsistent with the modal asymmetry of time in section 2.2, we saw that the problem arises from the relation of entailment between infallible foreknowledge and events in the future. We can see now that that it does not matter if the entailment is due to infallible foreknowledge. The content of the proposition in question does not matter. What matters is the entailment relation. The problem arises from any assumption that there is a proposition about the past that entails propositions about the future when combined with this kind of necessity. The deeper metaphysical problem is not about free will; it is not even about infallible foreknowledge.

The structure of fatalist arguments depends only upon temporally asymmetrical necessity, a transfer of necessity principle, and an entailment relation between past and future. It is the entailment between something in the past and something in the future that permits the fatalist to conclude that the future has the same necessity as the past, a conclusion that conflicts with the underlying Ockhamist assumption that the past and future are modally contrastive.

The problem is that it is impossible for there to be a type of modality that has the following features:

(i) The past and future are asymmetrical in that true propositions about the past are necessary with respect to this modality, whereas the true propositions about the future are contingent with respect to this modality.
(ii) The Transfer of Necessity Principle applies to this modality.
(iii) There are true propositions about the past that entail propositions about the future.

Propositions (i)–(iii) form an inconsistent triad, which can be demonstrated in the following argument.

Argument that accidental necessity/contingency is inconsistent with past/future entailment

Let *PAST* be a true proposition about the past. Assume that the past is now-necessary (accidentally necessary) and the future is now-contingent (accidentally contingent). Let *FUT* be a proposition about the future that is entailed by *PAST*.

(1) *PAST* is true. (Assumption)
(2) It is now-necessary that *PAST* is true. (Necessity of the Past)
(3) Necessarily (*PAST* is true -> *FUT* is true). (Assumption)
(4) It is now-necessary that *FUT* is true. (Transfer of Necessity Principle)

But by the Principle of the Contingency of the Future, we get

(5) It is now-contingent that *FUT* is true.

(5) contradicts (4).

As with the argument in stage 2, the above argument can be modified for those who wish to say that the modality of accidental necessity/contingency applies only to propositions that are not already necessary because of the causal structure of the world or metaphysical principles. On that interpretation, proposition *FUT* above would need to be a proposition about the future that is metaphysically and causally contingent. So, we have two interpretations of the scope of accidental necessity and contingency. With the interpretation I have said is the clearest and most persuasive, the conclusion is that a temporally asymmetrical modality like Ockham's accidental necessity/contingency with a transfer principle is inconsistent with the assumption that there are any propositions about the past that entail any propositions about the future. With the modified interpretation, the conclusion is that a temporally asymmetrical modality like Ockham's accidental necessity/contingency with a transfer principle is inconsistent with the assumption that there are propositions about the past that entail propositions about the metaphysically and causally contingent future. Either way, this is not a problem about free will or foreknowledge, but about time.

Let us look at possible examples of past-future entailments that are inconsistent with accidental necessity/contingency. Imagine the possibility of a necessarily enduring being, one that is neither metaphysically nor causally necessary, but if it exists, its nature is such that it necessarily continues to exist. Suppose, for example, that God does not exist necessarily. There are some possible worlds in which God does not exist, and God's existence is not caused by anything in the past. But let's imagine that if God exists in any world, God's nature is such that it is necessary that God continues to exist in that world. That is to say, necessarily, if God exists, God is everlasting. That assumption is inconsistent with the alleged modal asymmetry of time. Since p is true if and only if p, the argument can be given as follows:

(1) God existed in the past. (Assumption)
(2) It is now-necessary that God existed in the past. (Necessity of the Past)
(3) Necessarily, if God existed in the past, God will continue to exist in the future. (Assumption that God is necessarily everlasting)
(4) It is now-necessary that God will exist in the future. (Transfer of Necessity Principle)

By the Principle of the Contingency of the Future, we get

(5) It is now-contingent that God will exist in the future.

But (5) contradicts (4).

The existence of matter could be another example of a necessarily enduring being. Maybe matter is created by the choice of God, so it does not exist out of necessity, but God made it to be such that necessarily, once matter exists, it continues to exist until the end of time. Maybe matter and the sequence of time necessarily coexist because time is the measure of the motion of material objects. The Greek atomists had a theory of this kind. They maintained that there is nothing in the natural world but atoms and the void. Atoms persist throughout all time. I don't know if they would have said that the existence of an atom at one time entails its existence at later times, but I do not see anything incoherent about that theory. From another direction, Leibniz maintained that the only beings that are genuinely real are mind-like simple substances called monads, which cannot be destroyed. Again, I do not see anything incoherent in this theory, but these theories are incompatible with accidental necessity/contingency with a transfer principle, and the argument would be parallel to the above argument about a necessarily everlasting God.

There are also a multitude of examples of causally necessary relations between events in the past and events in the future. Even if causal determinism is false as a universal theory, few people would deny that there are necessary causal relations in nature. Human acts are said to be an exception, but for several hundred years, our scientific theories have maintained that given the laws of nature, there is a necessary connection between certain events at one point of time and certain subsequent events. If accidental contingency applies to the entire future, it applies to these events, and the entailment is inconsistent with the modal asymmetry of time.

Suppose instead that we adopt the second interpretation of accidental contingency mentioned above. Suppose that accidental contingency applies only to the metaphysically and causally contingent future. If so, there is an inconsistency among the following:

(i') The past and future are asymmetrical in that true propositions about the past are necessary with respect to this modality, whereas true propositions about the

metaphysically and causally contingent future are contingent with respect to this modality.
(ii') The Transfer of Necessity Principle applies to this modality.
(iii') There are true propositions about the past that entail propositions about the metaphysically and causally contingent future.

If we want to hang on to this interpretation of Ockham's distinction between accidental necessity and contingency, it needs to be clear that on pain of inconsistency, we may not propose the truth of any proposition about the past that entails a proposition about the metaphysically and causally contingent future, a restriction that is easy to overlook. We would be prevented from claiming that there is a God whose existence is metaphysically and causally contingent but is necessarily everlasting, and similarly for any other contingent but necessarily enduring being. It would also commit us to denying an entailment proposed by John Martin Fischer (1983) that *Jones sits at t1* entails *Jones does not sit for the first time at t2*. Similarly, *The Twin Towers were completed in 1971* entails *The Twin Towers were no more than thirty years old in 2001*. There are those who believe that every event in the future is causally necessary. If so, then as I have said, there is no point in making the distinction between accidental necessity and contingency at all. The same point applies if there is a true thesis that makes all of the future metaphysically necessary. Any such thesis vacates the content of accidental necessity/ contingency as given above.

At the beginning of this book, I remarked that since standard arguments for logical fatalism, theological fatalism, and causal fatalism are structurally the same, something must tie them together. I think we can see now that what ties them together is that they are all arguments that presuppose an entailment between a proposition about the past and a proposition about the future. But the three propositions used in those arguments are not the only ones we might postulate on the basis of theological, metaphysical, or scientific theories. Infallible foreknowledge is a well-known example of an entailment between past and future, but it is the entailment that is the problem, not the fact that it is a link between infallible foreknowledge and the lack of free will.

"But wait!" the contemporary Ockhamist will say. "We and Ockham are smart enough to make distinctions. Ockham cleverly argued that if a proposition about the past entails a proposition about the future, it is not *really* about the past. It is partly about the past and partly about the future. It is in the "soft" past. There is no inconsistency in (i)–(iii) or (i')–(iii') as long as we are clear that the principle of accidental necessity applies only to the hard past.[16] We agree that no proposition about the hard past entails a proposition about the future because, by definition, all such propositions are in the soft past.

This way of distinguishing the hard past from the soft past has a number of problems and is no longer accepted, but suppose that it could be made to work with qualifications. If so, it would hold out the promise of giving us a way to handle our trilemma. There is no inconsistency in the triad (i)–(iii) as long as we are clear about what is

---

[16] Ockham did not clearly distinguish the hard past from the soft past on the basis of an entailment relation, but the following passage is suggestive:

> Some propositions are about the present as regards both their wording and their subject matter. Where such [propositions] are concerned, it is universally true that every proposition about the present has [corresponding to it] a necessary one about the past—e.g., "Socrates is seated," "Socrates is walking," "Socrates is just," and the like.
>
> Other propositions are about the present as regards their wording only and are equivalently about the future, since their truth depends on the truth of propositions about the future. Where such [propositions] are concerned, the rule that every true proposition about the present has [corresponding to it] a necessary one about the past is not true. Ockham (1983), trans. Adams and Kretzmann, 46-47. [Words in brackets added by translators].

Note that Ockham refers to a proposition in the past that "depends on" a proposition about the future. He does not say "entails" as far as I can see, but that is a reasonable contemporary interpretation. Marilyn Adams (1967) adopts that interpretation. As I have said, subsequent Ockhamists have recognized that it is unsatisfactory as a way to distinguish the difference between the hard and soft past.

really past and what is really future as intended in the distinction between accidental necessity and contingency. Any proposition about the past that entails a proposition about the future and has the necessary qualifications is in the soft past.

So far so good, but what must this kind of Ockhamist say about causal determinism? If causal determinism is true, the conjunction of the laws of nature and the past history of the world entails all propositions about the future. It is logically necessary that given the state of the world in the past and universal laws of nature, the future will be what it will be. That means that given determinism and the Ockhamist line we are considering, all of the past is in the soft past. No proposition about the hard past entails a proposition about the future because there are no true propositions about the hard past. Presumably, most Ockhamists wish to deny the thesis of determinism, but the argument we have just seen has the consequence that they must reject the determinist thesis not only because of considerations about free will but also because it denies the modal asymmetry of time. Determinism means that God's past infallible beliefs are not an exception to the rule that most of the past is the hard past. There is no hard past.

Problems in the difference between hard and soft pasts will not surprise physicists whose physical theories are bi-directionally deterministic. For most physical theories, a specification of the state of the world at a time t, when combined with the laws, determines not only how things go after t but also how things go before t. What happens before or after t is equally determined by the state of the world at t in conjunction with physical laws.[17] The past is entailed by the future, and the future is entailed by the past. Using Ockhamist reasoning, that would mean that all of the future is in the soft future, and all of the past is in the soft past. There is no such thing as the hard past or the hard future.

---

[17] See discussion by Carl Hoefer (2023) in the *Stanford Encyclopedia of Philosophy* entry "Causal Determinism," section 2.3.

In the 1980s and 1990s, many papers defended Ockhamism by attempting to produce criteria distinguishing the hard past from the soft past that became more and more complicated to avoid counterexamples. As I mentioned, the attempt to make the distinction on the basis of entailment relations was given up.[18] The difficulty of separating the soft past from the hard past made another version of Ockhamism popular in this period. That was the idea that God's past beliefs are counterfactually dependent upon our acts, an idea I will discuss in Part Two. That version of Ockhamism is different from the version I have been discussing so far because it defines accidental necessity directly in terms of counterfactual power rather than by connecting accidental necessity to the hard past. I think we can say at a minimum that Ockhamism in any version opened a Pandora's box about the difference between past and future. We can conclude that if the difference between what is accidentally necessary and what is accidentally contingent is intended to map onto the difference between past and future, that difference must not permit any propositions about the real past to entail propositions about the real future without falling into inconsistency.

In this part of the book, we have seen that many solutions to fatalist arguments do not work against deeper arguments, but there is one solution that I have not yet discussed, and which we can now see is not sufficient to handle the dilemma of stage 3. That is the position that propositions about the contingent future have no truth value, a common solution to the dilemma of logical fatalism.

---

[18] Some of the defenses of this kind of Ockhamism in this period appear in Freddoso (1983), Kvanvig (1986), Wierenga (1989), and Craig (1990). Some of the criticisms appear in Fischer (1983), Hasker (1989), Widerker (1990), Zagzebski (1991), and Pike (1993). The Ockhamist strategy of distinguishing facts about the past that are really about the past and facts about the past that are in part about the future was later connected with work on the reality of the past and future. See Finch and Rea (2008) for an argument that the Ockhamist solution requires the rejection of presentism.

The argument for logical fatalism goes back to Aristotle's famous example of a future sea battle. Here is the argument with his example:

Argument for logical fatalism

(1) Yesterday the proposition *There will be a sea battle tomorrow* was true. (Assumption)
(2) It is now-necessary that yesterday *There will be a sea battle tomorrow* was true. (Necessity of the Past)
(3) Necessarily, if yesterday *There will be a sea battle tomorrow* was true, then there will be a sea battle tomorrow. (Meaning of "true")
(4) (2) and (3) entail that it is now-necessary that there will be a sea battle tomorrow. (Transfer of Necessity Principle)
(5) It is now-necessary that there will be a sea battle tomorrow. (2, 3, 4)

Aristotle had to find a way to reject this argument because not only would it have forced him to accept fatalism, it would have also forced him to give up his act/potency distinction. The sea battle tomorrow could be any future contingent event. He wanted to say that there is now a potency for that event to occur, and there is now a potency for it not to occur. The potency for its occurrence is reduced to act when the event occurs, and at that time, the potency for its non-occurrence is lost. If the potency for every event in the future has already been lost because of the nature of truth, the act/potency distinction is useless.

I have given a version of the argument for logical fatalism that has the same form as the argument for theological fatalism, but there is a possible difference that would alter the structure. It is not clear that the logical fatalist argument above needs the Transfer of Accidental Necessity principle rather than only a conversion of tenses. According to most theories of propositions, a proposition is the content of a sentence, and an appropriate change in the tense of the sentence does not change the proposition. The proposition expressed yesterday by "There will be a sea battle in two days" is the same proposition as the one expressed tomorrow by "There is a sea battle going on," and the same as the proposition expressed two days from now by "There was a sea battle yesterday." The sea battle argument without the transfer principle would go as follows:

(1′) Yesterday the proposition expressed by "There will be a sea battle in two days" was true. (Assumption)
(2′) It is now-necessary that the proposition expressed yesterday by "There will be a sea battle in two days" was true. (Necessity of the past)
(3′) The proposition expressed yesterday by "There will be a sea battle in two days" is the same as the proposition expressed tomorrow by "There is a sea battle going on now."
(4′) Therefore, it is now-necessary that the proposition expressed tomorrow by "There is a sea battle going on" is true.
(5′) If it is now-necessary that the proposition expressed tomorrow by "There is a sea battle going on" is true, then it is necessary that a sea battle will be going on tomorrow.

A common response to logical fatalist arguments is to deny (1′). Proposition (1′) can be denied either on the grounds that future contingents have no truth value or on the grounds that they are all false, as argued by Patrick Todd (2021). Notice that that also requires denying (3′). We would expect that even if future-tensed propositions are not true, the corresponding proposition in the present tense is true at the appropriate time. But I believe that this response is unnecessary and implausible. Ockham's distinction between truth and necessity is the answer. Now-true is not the same as now-necessary. Now-true does not affect the relation of potency and act, as I discussed in section 1. But whether or not the idea that future contingents are not true is a good way out of logical fatalism, does it help us with our deeper dilemmas?

The argument of this section leads us to the conclusion that there is an inconsistency between the idea of a temporally asymmetrical necessity (the past has it, the future does not) to which the Transfer of Necessity Principle applies if there is a true proposition about the past that entails a proposition about the future. Suppose for the sake of argument that no future contingent propositions are true. How would that help? The advocate of this way out would also have to deny entailment between any proposition about the past and a proposition about the future and, in addition, would have to deny that tensed propositions about the same event are the same proposition.[19] The denial of the truth of contingent propositions about the future does not solve the problem that there can be no entailments between past and future or, alternatively, between the past and the causally contingent future, and it adds the controversial position that propositions must be intrinsically tensed.

The necessity of the past demands our further attention, but what we have seen in this section is that the idea that there is a form of necessity that the past has because it is past and the future lacks because it is future is incompatible with the assumption that there are propositions about the past that entail propositions about the future. It was important to Ockham that not all of the future has already been reduced from potency to act for metaphysical or causal reasons. But it is worth repeating that if every event in the future is either metaphysically necessary or causally necessary, any reference to accidental necessity is superfluous.

There are propositions that are plausible for metaphysical, theological, or scientific reasons that have past-future entailments. Logical, theological, and causal fatalist arguments use these propositions, but there may be others, as I have pointed out. If we

---

[19] Patrick Todd's (2021) position is that future contingent propositions are false, and he accepts the lack of entailment between past and future propositions.

want to affirm any of these propositions, we must give up the idea of accidental necessity and contingency. I conclude that the inconsistency in (i)–(iii) shows that the idea of a temporally asymmetrical modality is incoherent. Any argument that uses this alleged form of necessity is a nonstarter.

We might wonder what motivates the idea of a temporally asymmetrical modality. I think that the answer is its connection to the arrow of time. There is more than one arrow, and I will discuss that in the next two parts, but a long history of fatalist arguments going back at least to Aristotle and Diodorus Cronus have been formulated in terms of the necessity of the past, a type of necessity that was often vague, but which got its plausibility from the idea that time has a modal arrow as well as a causal arrow and a psychological arrow. I have argued in this part of the book that a modal arrow does not make sense.

2.4. Conclusion to section 2: The incoherence of accidental necessity

The contrast between accidental necessity and accidental contingency is intuitive, but if we try to make it correspond to the logical modalities of necessity and contingency, we run into inconsistency. When we investigate historically important arguments for fatalism that interpret the necessity of the past as literally a form of necessity, we see an underlying incoherence. The arguments depend on an inconsistent or at best confused view about time. The problem in the modal arrow goes well beyond the connection between the modal arrow and fatalism.

Standard fatalist arguments implicitly assume a modal arrow of time in order to deny it. If the past is necessary, the argument goes, so is the future. But the assumption of the necessity of the past is plausible because it is one side of a modal arrow, the other side of which is the contingency of the future. That should alert us that there is a problem in our understanding of temporal arrows. The incoherence in the modal arrow is one reason we are confused about time. We will encounter others.

I will conclude this section by reviewing well-known responses to fatalist arguments that cannot handle one or more of the dilemmas we have uncovered. To begin, I should say that I would not be surprised if there is more than one mistake in the argument for theological fatalism, and if one of those responses works against that argument, that is a good thing. My purpose is to show that the existence of deeper dilemmas may make these responses unnecessary, and, in any case, the trilemma of this section shows that we need to address a problem in the logic of time. Let me review those responses.

First, there are the theological responses:

(a) The thesis that God and his beliefs are outside of time
(b) The thesis that God does not have beliefs
(c) My Thomistic Ockhamism
(d) Molinism

Each of these responses appeals to properties of God other than infallible foreknowledge, and therefore is inapplicable to the first stage of my reduction in section 2.1.

In the second stage of the argument in section 2.2, I showed that another response will not work against the argument of that section:

(e) The denial of the Principle of Alternate Possibilities

That principle in all its forms is only applicable to dilemmas about free will. The principle is useless against the argument that there is an inconsistency between infallible foreknowledge and the modal asymmetry of time. It also means that the Open Theism approach will not work for the dilemma in the logic of time given in that section.

In stage 3 we have seen that another response is unsatisfactory:

(f) The thesis that future contingents are not true, either because they are all false or because they have no truth value.

That solution is incompatible with the assumption that there are propositions about the past that entail propositions about the future. Of course, if we deny that assumption, the problem with the modal arrow of time disappears.

The only historically important response left is the Ockhamist solution. The Ockhamist hard fact/soft fact distinction does not misfire to the degree of the other solutions, but I believe that it overreaches. Suppose that you are attracted to the original Ockhamist position that no proposition about the past that entails a proposition about the future has the necessity of the past, and suppose that you can qualify it sufficiently to make it work. All such propositions are in the soft past. With that interpretation of the difference between the hard past and the soft past, the inconsistency identified here is avoided by denying that the modal asymmetry of time applies to these propositions. There are no propositions about the hard past that entail propositions about the hard future. The problem vanishes in one fell swoop. But the more we find entailments between past and future, the farther the Ockhamist division between past and future gets from the intuitive distinction between past and future. If the intention is to say that God's past beliefs are an exception to the idea that the past is accidentally necessary, it must not turn out that too many other propositions about the past are not accidentally necessary. As I mentioned, this version of the Ockhamist solution to theological fatalism has been given up for other reasons, and we will look at another solution that Alvin Plantinga traces to Ockham in Part Two. That solution defines accidental necessity/contingency directly in terms of human power rather than by an account of the distinction between past and future.

I conclude that the Ockhamist idea of accidental necessity and contingency is incoherent. It can be saved by denying that there are any true propositions about the past that entail propositions about the future, but that is a move that jeopardizes reasoning in many areas of philosophy that have nothing to do with fatalism. It jeopardizes theorizing in science and theology as well. We are used to focusing exclusively on fatalist arguments that arise from one particular premise connecting the past and future, but the denial of that premise reaches only as far as the domain of discourse from which it arises. The denial of divine infallibility is irrelevant to non-theists. The denial of causal necessitation between past and future can be ignored by those who are not interested in the literature on determinism. The alteration in the logic of propositions to avoid logical fatalism can be interpreted as a pedantic exercise of no interest to non-logicians. But if it turns out that the structure of time rules out the possibility of entailment between any proposition about the past and a proposition about the future, that is a severe constraint on theorizing in any area of human thought. Different people accept different entailment relations between past and future for different reasons, but if there is a modal arrow of time, all of them are mistaken. I conclude that there is no modal arrow of time, not because all events are equally fated, but because the idea of a modal arrow does not make sense.

The fatalist arguments I have presented hide a deep inconsistency. The modal arrow cannot be used to support fatalism because it hides the inconsistency uncovered in stage 2, but it is not only fatalists whose positions are incoherent. Non-fatalists who accept the fatalist argument until they get to the premise about free will also have an incoherent position. Furthermore, we are all muddled if we do not have a way to escape the inconsistency of stage 3. Of course, none of this shows that fatalism is false. It is the use of the idea of accidental necessity in the arguments for fatalism that is the problem. I conclude that the second premise of all the arguments I have discussed in this part of the book are false when interpreted in the Ockhamist way as one side of a modal arrow of time.

Section 3. Reactions and consequences

3.1. Can the conclusion be avoided?

Reply 1. "Forget Ockham. The intuition of the necessity of the past does not have to be tied to an arrow of time. When I speak of the necessity of the past, I am not thinking of Ockham's idea of necessity *per accidens,* where accidental necessity is a special kind of necessity that the past has in virtue of being past, and the future lacks in virtue of being future, and I do not connect it to Aristotle's idea of potency and act. I make no assumption about a modal arrow of time at the beginning of the argument. The past is necessary in virtue of being past, but the modal status of the future is up in the air. My point is that being past is sufficient for being necessary, where its necessity means that I cannot do anything about it. There are other reasons why some proposition or state of affairs is necessary. Maybe it is metaphysically necessary, or causally necessary, or it is entailed by something that is necessary in one of these senses. The future is entailed by certain propositions about the past that are necessary because they are past. The future is therefore necessary. That is all I mean to say in the fatalist argument."

If this response is correct, we could not get to stage 2 in section 2. Clearly, people who think that fatalism logically follows from the necessity of the past cannot consistently begin with the explicit premise that the future is non-necessitated. But that shows confusion in the formulation of the argument. What is it about the past that makes it necessary, and which is such that the future might or might not be necessary in the same sense? I have been assuming that like Aristotle and Ockham, we think of the necessity of the past as one side of a two-sided coin, where the other side is the contingency of the future. If someone says, "There is no use crying over spilled milk," and you ask, "Would you have said the same about the milk before it was spilled?" they will probably reply, "Of course not. The future is different. The past is finished and out of our control; the future has still to be created." But perhaps they hesitate. They might be convinced that the past is necessary, whether or not the future is also. They then follow the fatalist argument to its conclusion and discover that the future is just as necessary as the past. The coin of past and future has only one side. The conclusion is surprising, not only because fatalism is surprising, but also because the conclusion contradicts an admittedly vague idea about the difference between past and future with which the argument begins.

When people become convinced that the necessity of the past entails fatalism, they must rethink their original assumption about the necessity of the past. Can they retain their commitment to the necessity of the past *qua* past when they now believe that the future has the same necessity? I don't think that that is intelligible. If the past has a kind of necessity that accrues to the past in virtue of being past, the future cannot have *that* kind of necessity. The conclusion of the fatalist argument forces the fatalist to change something in the dialectic of the argument. At a minimum, they would have to conclude that what they initially called the necessity of the past is misnamed because it is not a necessity peculiar to the past, but it is the necessity of past, present, and future. It is necessity all the way through.

Fatalists end with a different conception of time than they had at the beginning. The issue I have raised is whether the end is consistent with the beginning. It is possible to make it consistent if the beginning intuition is vague enough, but at a minimum, that demands attention. It is fair for the skeptic about accidental necessity to ask the fatalist or non-fatalist defender of accidental necessity: "What, exactly, is this necessity that you are so sure the past has, and the future might or might not have? What are the grounds for the difference between your certainty that the past has it, and your neutrality about its possession by the future?" The defender of this version of the necessity of the past might have an answer, but it is not something that I see in fatalist arguments. That also means that the kind of anti-fatalist who believes that we *would* be committed to the necessity of everything in time if we accept the starting premise concedes too much. We should all ask the fatalist to make it clear what we are accepting about the arrow of time before the argument begins.

If necessity attaches to the past *qua* past, the future cannot have that kind of necessity. However, the defender of this way out of my argument could move to another way of thinking about the modality of time that ties past and future together through a different transfer principle than the one used in the arguments of this part of the book. Suppose they say: "Well, I admit that I don't know what kind of necessity the past has, but I believe that the past has some kind of necessity, and other events, including events in the future, are necessary for other reasons. We can infer the necessity of the future if we adopt a broad transfer of necessity principle that goes like this: If p is necessary in some sense or other, and p entails q, then q is necessary in some sense or other. It does not matter if the future is necessary in the same sense as the past. All I need for the fatalist argument to succeed is that the future is necessary in some sense, a sense that is like the past in that alternatives have been ruled out."

Notice first that this reply admits a lack of clarity about what the necessity of the past is and whether it includes an implied arrow, as I have argued. Notice next that the broadening of the transfer principle moves it further from Axiom K, the axiom that is the logical pivot in standard fatalist arguments, and for that reason, the revised transfer principle is not as well supported by the formal credentials of the fatalist arguments we have investigated so far. The broadening of the transfer principle differs from what we have considered in this part of the book. It will reappear in Peter van

Inwagen's consequence argument that determinism entails fatalism in Part Two.

This response reveals how muddled we are about what the necessity of the past amounts to, and how hard it is to agree about that. Intuitions about fatalist arguments differ in part because the starting intuitions differ. The reply to my argument that we are looking at now detaches the necessity of the past from an arrow of time. The suggestion is to forget Ockham because he mistakenly tied the necessity of the past to a modal arrow. I agree that we need to forget Ockham, but for a different reason. His idea of accidental necessity faces the trilemmas I have described. However, that still leaves us with the question, "What is the necessity of the past?" At least Ockham had the advantage of an account of accidental necessity that was connected to the metaphysics of change, and it permitted an explanation of the difference between truth and necessity in response to logical fatalist arguments. What I see in this discussion is that the necessity of the past needs to be re-examined. In Part Two I will give an interpretation of the necessity of the past as the causal closure of the past. But that idea also has a temporal arrow that we will need to investigate.

Reply 2. A very different reaction to my conclusion can come from the anti-fatalist direction, and it would undermine all the arguments we have examined. The inconsistent triad (i)–(iii) can be resolved if the transfer of necessity principle does not apply to accidental necessity. Recall that in her introduction to Ockham's work on foreknowledge and predestination, Marilyn Adams (Ockham 1983) says that it is important that the kind of necessity Ockham is talking about is "real" temporal necessity, not logical necessity. Adams does not mention the Transfer of Necessity Principle, but it is clearly a principle of logic that requires accidental necessity to be treated the same way as logical necessity. Can the transfer principle be denied if Ockham's temporal modality is not like logical modalities?

Let's look at how this move would have to go. If *p* is now-necessary, that means that there is now a lack of potency for *not p*. If *p* entails *q*, can we deny that it follows that there is now a lack of potency for *not q*? It would be hard to get that to work. The denial of the transfer principle is more plausible if accidental necessity is not really a form of necessity, but the metaphysical basis for the difference between past and future would require much more clarification. Suppose we leave out the term "necessity" and speak only in terms of act and potency. If God's beliefs about the future were always in act, it seems to follow that the future was always in act. If not, we need more than a simple denial of the Transfer of Necessity Principle to explain it.[20] We need a robust theory of the nature of "real" versus "logical" modalities to back it up.

Reply 3. So far, I have mentioned two ways of avoiding the inconsistency in the conjunction of (i), (ii), and (iii). Assumption (i) is that there is a temporally asymmetrical modality that distinguishes past from future. The past is necessary in this sense; the future is contingent in this sense. The first response is to deny that accidental necessity is temporally asymmetrical. The past has it, the future may or may not have it. Assumption (ii) is that the Transfer of Necessity Principle applies to this kind of necessity. I have suggested that perhaps that assumption can be denied if we distinguish "real" necessity from necessity as used by logicians. Assumption (iii) is that there are propositions about the past that entail propositions about the future. Assumptions (i) and (ii) can be saved by denying that there is any proposition about the "real" past that entails a proposition about the "real" future. Some philosophers may be willing to take this line, but I am interpreting it as a last resort. We have also seen the position of early contemporary Ockhamists who distinguished the real past from the soft or quasi-past, and they did so by

---

[20] I discussed examples that could be used to reject the Transfer of Necessity Principle in Zagzebski (1991), Chapter 6, section 2.2. The kind of necessity that is being transferred is relevant, and there may be different senses of the necessary or the unavoidable or the nonaccidental that do not satisfy the transfer principle.

claiming that no proposition about the past that entails a proposition about the future is in the real past. That solves the problem by giving a reinterpretation of past and future. I grant that if there are a few propositions about the past that turn out to be in the soft past, we probably could live with that. But the more there are, the more the distinction between accidental necessity and contingency fails to map onto the distinction between past and future in any intuitive sense. When we speak of arrows of time, we think of the psychological arrow, which is the arrow of human experience, and we may think of the arrow of the expansion of the universe and the thermodynamic arrow. Is the modal arrow as modified by the Ockhamist an arrow of the same thing as these other arrows? How should we think about time if the different arrows of time do not line up?

The responses to my arguments so far need a hearing, and I have mentioned them only briefly because I think that all of them border on desperation moves to avoid the inconsistency in the conjunction of (i)–(iii). Even the Ockhamist idea of the difference between the real or hard past and what is only apparently about the past is a kind of desperation move because it is the sort of theory that a clever philosopher creates when up against a wall. Walls are everywhere in philosophy, and I think that sometimes the best move is to start over from the beginning before we get enmeshed in a philosophical maze.

3.2. Conclusion to Part One

Fatalism is threatening, or at least bothersome. It is bothersome enough that it has led philosophers since antiquity to carefully produce logically valid arguments for it and then to try to find a way to escape the arguments if they can. From the time of Aristotle up to the 21st century, the problem was interpreted as a puzzle about time and modal logic, the topic of this part of the book. Standard arguments for logical fatalism, theological fatalism, and causal fatalism have been formulated in parallel ways, arising from the combination of the necessity of the past and a transfer of necessity principle. But I have argued that these arguments have an even deeper structure that is not about fatalism. I do not like the possibility that we do not have free will, but the problem with the fatalist arguments we have examined is not fundamentally about our free will and what we like or dislike. It is about the logical structure of time and its connection to entailments between past and future.

I think that we are confused about time, and we are especially confused about the relation between past and future. Possibly that difference is an illusion, but it is natural to think that time moves away from the past and toward the future. We think that that has implications for our power over the future, and that it connects with other arrows of time in physics and in metaphysics. In Part Two I will go back to the beginning, to the assumption of the necessity of the past, and I will examine the idea that it is not what Ockham thought about the past, and it is not a form of necessity.

Part Two
Fatalism and the Causal Structure of Time

Section 1. Revisiting the necessity of the past

1.1. The causal closure of the past and fatalist arguments

What is left of the necessity of the past? Do we know that there is any such thing? If we give up the idea that the so-called necessity of the past is a form of necessity like Ockham's necessity *per accidens*, we still have the intuition that the past is outside our control. The past is causally closed. By that I mean that nothing now can either cause or prevent what has already happened. But it is not pastness in itself that puts something outside the realm of our causal power. It is pastness plus the metaphysical law that causes must precede their effects. In section 1 I will look at what happens to fatalist arguments when they are reformulated in terms of the causal closure of the past. In section 2 I will look at the possibility of backward causation or its obscure cousin, counterfactual power over the past.

It is hard to know what ordinary people believe, but it is unlikely that people who say that there is no use crying over spilled milk mean to say that the past is "necessary" in the sense in which the necessary can be inter-defined in standard ways with the possible, the impossible, and the contingent. If a proposition *p* is necessary, *p* is possible, but if milk was spilled, do ordinary people say that the proposition *Milk was spilled* is possible? The negation of a necessary truth is impossible, but would they say that *Milk was spilled* is necessary, and *Milk was not spilled* is impossible? They might, but it would be very unnatural to say such things. What is more likely is that both *Milk was spilled* and *Milk was not spilled* are put in the category of what we cannot do anything about. We can neither cause the past spilling of milk nor prevent it from being spilled. Both the actual past and alternative pasts are beyond our causal power. In fact, actual and counterfactual pasts are beyond the causal power of anything, not just human agents. If that is right, ordinary intuition supports my contention that the idea of the necessity of the past is not about accidental necessity. It is the idea that the past is causally closed.

A test of whether I am right in this conjecture is the intuitive response to a world in which there is backward causation. What would we say about the necessity of the past in that world? Would we say that the past has a kind of necessity in virtue of being past even though it is possible to cause what has already happened or to prevent what has already happened? I doubt it. Without a causal arrow, there would be no adage about spilled milk. Of course, maybe we cannot make sense of such a world at all. I am not denying that. My point is only that I do not see anything in addition to the denial that there is such a world in the idea of the necessity of the past.

My interpretation of the "necessity" of the past as the causal closure of the past retains an important difference between past and future. They are contrasted in that if some event E is in the past, E is not now causable, and not E is not now causable. If some event E is in the future, E is now causable by something, and it is at least arguable that not E is causable by something. Whether an alternative future is causable takes us directly to the fatalist problem, but we need not take a stand on that to see that there is a causal asymmetry between past and future as long as the future is causable and the past is not. There is a causal arrow of time.

Using this interpretation of the necessity of the past, we can reformulate the fatalist arguments of Part One. Let me begin with a definition and two principles.

Definition of causal closure

> Event E is causally closed $=_{df}$ There is nothing now that can cause E, and there is nothing now that can cause not E.

We will need to replace the principle of the necessity of the past with the following principle:

Principle of the Causal Closure of the Past

> If E is an event in the past, E is causally closed.

We will also need to replace the Transfer of Accidental Necessity Principle with the following:

Transfer of Causal Closure Principle

> If E occurs and is causally closed, and if necessarily, if E occurs then F occurs, then F occurs (or will occur) and is causally closed.

The fatalist arguments from causal closure are structurally parallel to the arguments of Part One.

Argument for theological fatalism from causal closure

(1) God infallibly believed yesterday that S will do A tomorrow. (Assumption)

From the principle of the causal closure of the past we get:

(2) God's believing yesterday that S will do A tomorrow is causally closed.

From the definition of divine infallibility we get:

(3) Necessarily, if God believed yesterday that S will do A tomorrow, then S will do A tomorrow.

From 2, 3, and the Transfer of Causal Closure Principle, we get:

(4) S will do A tomorrow and it is causally closed that S will do A tomorrow.

From the definition of causal closure, we can conclude:

(5) If S will do A tomorrow and it is causally closed that S will do A tomorrow, then S cannot cause it to happen that S does not do A tomorrow.

The Principle of Alternate Possibilities (PAP) states:

(6) If S cannot cause it to happen that S does not do A tomorrow, then S will not do A tomorrow freely.

By 4, 5, 6, and hypothetical syllogism we conclude:

(7) S will not do A tomorrow freely.

Argument for logical fatalism from the causal closure of the past

(1) Yesterday it was true that S will do A tomorrow. (Assumption)

From the principle of the causal closure of the past we get:

(2) The fact that it was true yesterday that S will do A tomorrow is causally closed.

From the definition of "true" we get:

(3) Necessarily, if it was true yesterday that S will do A tomorrow, then S will do A tomorrow.

From 2, 3, and the Transfer of Causal Closure Principle, we can infer:

(4) S will do A tomorrow and it is causally closed that S will do A tomorrow.

From the definition of causal closure we deduce:

(5) If S will do A tomorrow and it is causally closed that S will do A tomorrow, then S cannot cause it to happen that S does not do A tomorrow.

The Principle of Alternate Possibilities states:

(6) If S cannot cause it to happen that S does not do A tomorrow, then S will not do A tomorrow freely.

By 4, 5, 6, and hypothetical syllogism we can conclude:

(7) S will not do A tomorrow freely.

Argument for causal fatalism from the causal closure of the past
Let H = the total past history of the world, L = the universal causal laws. Assume that it is true that S will do A tomorrow. Assume causal determinism: Necessarily, if H and L, then S will do A tomorrow.

(1) Yesterday it was true that H and L. (Assumption)

From the Principle of the Causal Closure of the Past we get:

(2) It is now causally closed that H and L.

The thesis of causal determinism tells us:

(3) Necessarily, if H and L, then S will do A tomorrow.

From 2, 3, and the Transfer of Causal Closure Principle we can infer:

(4) S will do A tomorrow and it is causally closed that S will do A tomorrow.

From the definition of causal closure we deduce:

(5) If S will do A tomorrow and it is causally closed that S will do A tomorrow, then S cannot cause it to happen that S does not do A tomorrow.

The Principle of Alternate Possibilities states:

(6) If S cannot cause it to happen that S does not do A tomorrow, then S will not do A tomorrow freely.

By 4, 5, 6, and hypothetical syllogism we can conclude:

(7) S will not do A tomorrow freely.

These arguments have two important differences from the arguments of Part One. Although structurally identical to those arguments, both the change from the accidental necessity of the past to the causal closure of the past, and the change from the Transfer of Accidental Necessity Principle to the Transfer of Causal Closure Principle alters the arguments in significant ways.

First, let us look at the second premise of the three arguments. These premises refer to the causal closure of something that is probably not in the causal domain, and they then argue that what that entails is causally closed. Whatever the relation is between God's beliefs and our acts, it is doubtful that it is causal. Similarly, we are told in line (2) of the logical fatalist argument that the fact that it was true yesterday that S will do A tomorrow is causally closed. But it is very unlikely that the relation between an act and the truth of the abstract object expressing the occurrence of that act is causal. The same point applies to the second premise of the causal argument. Past concrete events are caused, but what about causal laws? The problem here is that something outside the causal realm can entail something within the causal realm over which we have causal power. The fact that $2 + 2 = 4$ is presumably outside the causal realm, and it entails that anybody who puts two green apples and two red apples in a basket thereby puts four apples in the basket. But that does not deprive Ann of the causal power to put four apples in her basket by putting two green and two red apples in her basket.

Another example comes from Plato. Plato maintained that the world of Forms is eternal and uncaused. Nobody has causal power over the Forms. The Form Beauty entails that all the inferior beautiful things in the world are beautiful, including the beauty of an enchanting painting. But the artist caused the painting to be beautiful even though its beauty is entailed by the Form Beauty. The relation between the Forms and the sensible world does not prevent normal causal relations from obtaining in the sensible world.

I am not suggesting that the problem with this premise is enough to lead us to dismiss the arguments, but it is enough to show us that the connection between the relation of causal power and the entailment relation is not straightforward.

The second difference between the new arguments and the arguments in Part One is the formulation of the Transfer of Causal Closure Principle as used in all three arguments. That principle does not have the force of logic, so it is more open to criticism than the Transfer of Accidental Necessity Principle. But more importantly, the Transfer of Causal Closure Principle licenses the inference to (4), and (4) denies that there are causes of the future. Most of us assume that it is uncontroversial that something now, whether agents or events, can cause future events.

This issue arises because the Principle of the Causal Closure of the Past has two conjuncts. One is the following:

Principle of the Non-causability of the Past

If E is an event in the past, nothing now can cause E.

The relevant half of the transfer of causal closure principle for this conjunct is the following:

Transfer of Non-causability Principle

If E occurs and is now non-causable, and if necessarily, if E occurs then F occurs, then F occurs (will occur) and is now non-causable.

But nobody would argue as follows:

(1) Suppose God believed yesterday that S will do A tomorrow.

From the Principle of the Non-causability of the Past, we get:

(2) There is nothing now that can cause God to have believed yesterday that S will do A tomorrow.

(3) Necessarily, if God believed yesterday that S will do A tomorrow, then S will do A tomorrow.

Therefore,

(4) S will do A tomorrow, and there is nothing now that can cause S to do A tomorrow.

Presumably (4) is false because (4) denies that there are causes of events in the future.

On the other hand, if we take just the second half of the principle of the causal closure of the past, we get an argument for fatalism that many philosophers treat seriously:

Principle of the Unpreventability of the Pastrin

If E is an event in the past, nothing now can cause not E.

The relevant half of the Transfer of Causal Closure Principle gives us the following:

Transfer of Unpreventability Principle

If E occurs and it is now non-causable that E does not occur, and if necessarily, if E occurs then F occurs, then F occurs and it is now non-causable that F does not occur.

This principle is virtually identical to the Transfer of Unpreventability Principle proposed by Hugh Rice (2005) in his response to a paper of mine. In the contemporary literature, it goes back to A. N. Prior (1962, 18). The principle is also close to a version of Peter van Inwagen's well-known rule Beta, which he uses in his Consequence Argument that causal determinism is incompatible with human free will. I will discuss rule Beta and the Consequence argument in the next section.

Using the Principle of the Unpreventability of the Past, we get a different argument for theological fatalism.

Argument for theological fatalism from the unpreventability of the past

(1) Suppose God believed yesterday that S will do A tomorrow.

From the Principle of the Unpreventability of the Past we get:

(2) There is nothing now that can prevent God from believing yesterday that S will do A tomorrow.

From the definition of divine infallibility, we know:

(3) Necessarily, if God believed yesterday that S will do A tomorrow, then S will do A tomorrow.

From 2, 3, and the Transfer of Unpreventability Principle, we get:

(4) S will do A tomorrow and there is nothing now that can cause S not to do A tomorrow.

From a variation of the Principle of Alternate Possibilities, we know:

(5) If nothing can cause S not to do A tomorrow, then S does not do A tomorrow freely.

From 4 and 5, we conclude:

(6) S does not do *A* tomorrow freely.

The parallel arguments for logical fatalism and causal fatalism are straightforward.

Argument for logical fatalism from the unpreventability of the past

(1) Suppose it was true yesterday that S will do A tomorrow.
(2) There is nothing now that can prevent it from being true yesterday that S will do A tomorrow.
(3) Necessarily, if it was true yesterday that S will do A tomorrow, then S will do A tomorrow.

From 2, 3, and the Transfer of Unpreventability Principle, we get:

(4) S will do A tomorrow and there is nothing now that can cause S not to do A tomorrow.

From a variation of the Principle of Alternate Possibilities, we get:

(5) If nothing can cause S not to do A tomorrow, then S does not do A tomorrow freely.

From 4 and 5, we conclude:

(6) S does not do A tomorrow freely.

Argument for causal fatalism from the unpreventability of the past

(1) Yesterday it was true that H and L. (Assumption)

From the Principle of the Unpreventability of the Past we get:

(2) The fact that it was true yesterday that H and L is now unpreventable.

The thesis of causal determinism tells us:

(3) Necessarily, if H and L, then S will do A tomorrow.

From 2, 3, and the Transfer of Unpreventability Principle we infer:

(4) S will do A tomorrow and there is nothing now that can cause S not to do A tomorrow.

From a variation of the Principle of Alternate Possibilities, we get:

(5) If nothing can cause S not to do A tomorrow, then S does not do A tomorrow freely.

From 4 and 5, we conclude:

(6) S does not do A tomorrow freely.

Taken in isolation, these arguments have convinced many people, although the problem with combining premise (2) and the transfer principle still needs to be addressed. But aside from that difficulty, I have pointed out a feature of all three arguments that should make us suspicious. They argue for fatalism by using *one half* of the Principle of the Causal Closure of the Past, where the other half conflicts with the existence of causes of the future and presumably is false.

The causal closure of the past expresses the causal arrow, which says that the past can be neither caused nor prevented. Nobody can cause it to happen, and nobody can cause it not to happen. But half of the principle leads to the denial that there are causes of the future. Licensing a transfer principle for the uncausability of the past leads to the uncausability of the future, and most people think it is obvious that the future is causable by something. That principle is not mentioned in fatalist arguments, which suggests that even fatalists consider it implausible. The transfer principle for the unpreventability of the past is the governing principle in the argument, and the Transfer of Uncausability Principle is cunningly left aside. But why accept one half of the causal closure of the past and not the other? If those who think that the actual future is causable take that to be a reason to deny the Transfer of Non-causability Principle, then it seems to me that those who think that alternative futures are causable have reason to deny the Transfer of Unpreventability Principle. At a minimum, the explanation for the difference in the two principles needs to be addressed. The Transfer of Unpreventability Principle cannot be based on a false transfer of causal closure.

Here is a reply I would expect. "Well, we all agree that something can cause the future, so the Transfer of Non-causability Principle is invalid, but we do not agree that something can cause alternate futures, and so the Transfer of Unpreventability Principle cannot be rejected on the grounds that all agree that it endorses inference from a truth to a falsehood." But this answer cuts both ways. It makes it clear that the fatalist conclusion of the preceding argument is not something to which we are forced by principles we all endorse. Rather, the transfer principle that endorses the fatalist conclusion is as disputable as fatalism. The uncausability of the past and the unpreventability of the past are both part of the same intuition that the past is causally closed. Neither transfer principle is a principle of logic like the Transfer of Necessity Principle, and both principles license an inference to a metaphysical conclusion that is unacceptable to most or many people. It seems to me that more needs to be said about what is going on in the intuition of the causal closure of the past. It is not enough to note that the argument supports fatalism when half of the intuition generating the argument has consequences that are unacceptable to most people.

Can we justify dividing the causal closure of the past into two? One half is that there is no backward causation. The other half is that there is no backward prevention. The first half is that we cannot make something exist in the past; the second half is that we cannot prevent something from existing in the past. Either there is something there in the past or there is not. If it is there, we cannot now make it go out of existence. If it is not there, we cannot now make it come into existence. The causal history of events in the past is already completed. Why think, then, that since we cannot prevent something in the past, we cannot prevent something in the future entailed by it, but deny that since we cannot cause the past, we cannot cause something in the future entailed by it? One would think that these transfer principles stand or fall together. They constitute an intuitive package about the causal arrow.

The causal closure of the past makes the principle that we cannot cause something to happen in the past that did not happen as strong as the principle that we cannot prevent something from happening in the past that did happen. If an accident has already occurred, there is no use trying to prevent it. Likewise, if we forgot an important appointment, there is no use trying to keep it now. The causal arrow means that we are causally blocked from affecting the past whether or not a past event actually happened. We cannot make something happen in the past that didn't happen, and we cannot make something happen in the past that *did* happen. The causes have already occurred. In the same way, we cannot prevent something from happening that did happen, and we cannot prevent something from happening that didn't happen. If the milk did not spill, we cannot now cause it not to spill. The causes that led to its not spilling have already occurred. There is a wall of causation separating causal forces from the past. That is what we mean by the causal arrow.

Let's look at how this problem connects with determinism. Suppose that determinism is true. That means that whether something happens or does not happen is determined by a chain that goes back to causal events in the distant past. I can no more cause what is entailed by the past than prevent it. The Transfer of Non-causability Principle and the Transfer of Preventability Principle go together, and the fatalist conclusion should be that it is now too late to cause or prevent anything in the future.

The same point holds if the occurrence or non-occurrence of events in the future is entailed by divine foreknowledge rather than laws of causality. Suppose that I can neither make God have a belief in the past nor prevent God from having a belief in the past. What should we say about the transfer principles? Would there be any difference in my power to do what is entailed by what God believes than to prevent it? If the transfer of causal closure holds for preventing what is entailed by God's beliefs, it ought to hold for causing what is entailed by God's beliefs.

I believe that the defender of the fatalist argument above should accept that the two principles go together. Whether the future is entailed by causal determinism or by infallible foreknowledge, nothing now can cause anything, whether in the past or in the future. The future was determined at the beginning of time or before the beginning of time, and that was the end of it.

Let's look now at how the fatalist argument from the unpreventability of the past uses the causal arrow. In Part One I argued that the fatalist argument from infallible foreknowledge presupposes the modal arrow and then uses it to argue that there is no modal arrow. The argument for causal fatalism does the same thing. The causal closure of the past gets its plausibility because of the presumption of the causal arrow, but the argument then uses it to argue that there isn't a causal arrow because the future is as causally closed as the past.

I conclude that the argument for fatalism from the unpreventability of the past has at least two problems. One is that the unpreventability of the past is plausible only because it is half of the causal closure of the past, where the other half has the consequence that there are no causes of the future. However, that might be acceptable to a defender of the argument. The second problem is that the argument appears to assume the causal arrow in order to deny it. Is there a causal arrow or not? If there is not, the intuition underlying the premise of the causal closure of the past needs to be addressed for the same reason the intuition underlying the necessity of the past in the arguments of Part One needs to be addressed. The arguments waffle between the idea of the necessity of the past *qua* past and its rejection.

1.2. The consequence argument against determinism

The Principle of the Unpreventability of the Past, in one form or another, took center stage in arguments about determinism. The change from the dominance of the modal arguments of Part One to the causal arguments of this part of the book is historically interesting because the change of focus was not due to general agreement that the modal arguments failed. Rather, the causal arguments became influential because they were a direct hit on our causal power, and at least superficially did not require the Principle of Alternate Possibilities, a key premise in the starting argument of Part One. The argument I will discuss here is called the Consequence Argument for the incompatibility of determinism and free will. It became one of the most important arguments for the position that determinism entails fatalism. The argument proceeds from the assumption that the history of the world in the distant past when combined with the laws of nature have the consequence that only one future is possible—the actual one. Peter van Inwagen (1983) expressed this point in his influential book on free will in terms of what is "up to us":

> If determinism is true, then our acts are the consequence of laws of nature and events in the remote past. But it's not up to us what

went on before we were born, and neither is it up to us what the laws of nature are. Therefore, the consequences of these things (including our present acts) are not up to us. (56)

In the formal presentation of his argument, Van Inwagen first introduces a modal operator defined as follows:

Np abbreviates "p, and no one has, or every had, any choice about whether p" (93).

He then proposes two inference rules contained in the logic of the N operator, where ⊃ is the material conditional:

Alpha: From Nec p, we may infer Np.
Beta: From Np and N (p ⊃ q), we may infer Nq. (94)

Rule Beta is similar to our Transfer of Causal Closure Principle.[1]

Assume determinism: Nec [(H & L) ⊃ F], where F is any event in the future you like. As before, we will use the event that S does A tomorrow as our example.

First consequence argument for the incompatibility of determinism and free will

(1) Nec [(H & L) ⊃ S does A tomorrow] From determinist thesis
(2) Nec [H ⊃ (L ⊃ S does A tomorrow)]
    by exportation
(3) N [H ⊃ (L ⊃ S does A tomorrow)]
    by rule Alpha
(4) N H premise

---

[1] I have used that principle in the form of an axiom modeled on an axiom of modal logic. The difference between an axiom and an inference rule does not affect the logical force of the argument and can be ignored in this context. For an elegant axiomatic version of symbolic logic, see Alonzo Church's (1996) classic *Introduction to Mathematical Logic*, which contains only one rule of inference and rules of substitution.

(5) N (L ⊃ S does A tomorrow)
    3, 4 by rule Beta
(6) N L premise
(7) N S does A tomorrow
    5, 6 by rule Beta[2]

An interesting feature of this argument is that the operator N is not a logical operator or a quasi-logical operator. It is an operator about human power. As we will see, that permits Van Inwagen to avoid the steps in the fatalist arguments that explicitly refer to the Principle of Alternate Possibilities.

Rule Beta is invalid, but Van Inwagen (2000) argues that it can be fixed.[3] He proposes to alter the N operator to the following: Np = "p, and no one can or ever could do anything such that if she did it, the proposition p might be false." This new operator gives a counterfactual interpretation of human power, and we will discuss that in the next section. An easier fix is the one proposed by Finch and Warfield (1998). They propose strengthening rule Beta to Beta 2: Np & Nec (p → q), then Nq. I will use Beta 2 below.

Rule Beta generated a large literature, but my interest is not in the formulation of the rule but in a peculiarity of the N operator itself. There are many things that we do not have and never had any choice about, including laws of nature and logic, as well as, presumably, the past. The reason we lack power over laws of nature or logic differs from the reason we lack power over the past. This difference affects the plausibility of rule Beta.

---

[2] The above argument is based on the argument Van Inwagen gives with different symbols (1983, 93–95). It is close to the version given by Kadri Vihvilen (2022) in her entry "Arguments for Incompatibilism" in the *Stanford Encyclopedia of Philosophy*.

[3] The problem is that rule Beta entails agglomeration, as shown by McKay and Johnson (1996), and agglomeration is invalid. That is the inference from Np and Nq to N(p & q). Timothy O'Connor (1993) suggests adding that p is made true earlier than q to avoid other counterexamples. Adding that clause does not affect the arguments discussed here since all the arguments are of cases in which p is made true earlier than q.

Rule Beta applied to logic or laws of nature is highly plausible.[4] Rule Beta as applied to the past is more complicated. I believe that it gets its plausibility from a combination of the idea that the past is causally closed to us with the idea that human power is about causal closure. So, I propose that the claim "no one has, or every had, any choice about whether p" is the conjunction of three ideas:

(a) No one could ever cause it to be the case that p.
(b) No one could ever cause it to be the case that not p.
(c) A choice about whether p is the ability to cause it to be the case that p or to cause it to be the case that not p.

In this analysis, I am interpreting the causal relation broadly, including indirect causation and partial causation. We say that no one has or ever had any choice about whether p when they could never directly cause it to be the case that p or not p, nor could they exercise causal influence over the direct cause, such as influencing someone else's causal power. This analysis means that the Consequence Argument for the incompatibility of determinism and free will is partly the same as the argument for fatalism from the causal closure of the past discussed in the last section.

Let's look at what happens to the Consequence Argument when we keep the separate elements of the N operator in mind. Conjunct (c) tells us that nobody has any choice about whether p unless they can either cause it to be the case that p or cause it to be the case that not p. If we apply conjunct (a) to the past, that leads to the conclusion that nobody can cause the future. Applying conjunct (b) leads to the conclusion that nobody can prevent the future. The first option licenses an inference that is fallacious if there are causes of the future. The second option implicitly uses the Principle of Alternate

---

[4] But David Lewis (1981) argues that I am able to do something such that, if I did it, a law would be broken. However, he denies the stronger thesis that I am able to break a law.

Possibilities (PAP). Rule Beta therefore reduces to a debate about that principle. It is PAP that is doing the real work in the argument.

In Part One section 2.3, I argued that standard fatalist arguments reduce to a trilemma. Accidental necessity and contingency do not make sense when combined with theses of entailment between past and future. For that reason, I concluded that the idea of accidental necessity is incoherent, and the most plausible interpretation of the necessity of the past is that the past is causally closed. Does that change escape the problem of Part One?

I think not. With the change, we are confronted with parallel trilemmas in combining the causal arrow of time, the Transfer of Non-causability Principle or Van Inwagen's rule Beta, and causal determinism.

First trilemma
Let's first interpret the causal arrow as the principle that the future is causable; the past is not. There is then an inconsistency among the following:

(1) The causal arrow
Causes exist (and existed in the past) and operate in a forward direction, not a backward direction. Past events are non-causable. Future events are causable. Laws of causality are non-causable.
(2) Transfer of Non-causability Principle
If E occurs and is now non-causable, and if necessarily, if E occurs then F occurs, then F occurs and is now non-causable.
(3) Determinist thesis: Necessarily, the conjunction of past events and causal laws entails the future.

Since (1) tells us that the past and the laws are non-causable, it follows from the determinist thesis and the Transfer of Non-causability Principle that the future is non-causable. But (1) says that the future is causable.

Suppose we use the Transfer of Unpreventability Principle instead. If the causal arrow means that the past is unpreventable and the future is not unpreventable, we get a straightforward contradiction among:

(1) The causal arrow—the past is unpreventable, the future is not unpreventable
(2) Transfer of Unpreventability Principle
(3) Causal determinism

The determinist knows that and does not start by assuming an arrow of preventability. That arrow is left up in the air, and if so, it should be explicit that there is no assumption of a preventability arrow. But then we have the same problem faced by the defender of the modal arrow in Part One. Why insist that the past is unpreventable unless there is something about the past *qua* past that makes it unpreventable, in which case the future *qua* future is not unpreventable in the same way? If the unpreventability of the past is tied to its pastness, it looks like there is a temporal arrow of preventability, in which case we get another contradiction. Whichever way we go on this issue, we face a problem that is not about free will. It is a problem with our notion of causability in general and our lack of clarity about the causal arrow of time, if there is any such thing.

Second trilemma

Let us look at the problem when we substitute a plausible version of the N operator for thesis (2) above. Following the way I have unpacked the N operator, let Np = p, and nobody now has any choice about whether p because (i) nobody now can do anything that causes it to be the case that p, and (ii) nobody now can do anything that causes it to be the case that not p, and (iii) nobody now has any choice about whether p unless they can either cause it to be the case that p or cause it to be the case that not p.

The Beta principle modified above to Beta 2 is this:

Beta2: Np and necessarily (p -> q) /: Nq

We can see now that there is an inconsistency in the following:

(1) Causal arrow
(2) Beta2 principle
(3) Determinist thesis—same as above

The Consequence Argument and the more general fatalist arguments from the non-causability and unpreventability of the past highlight underlying issues about the direction of causation and the relation between cause and effect. We need to decide whether there is a causal arrow or not. If there is no arrow, the connection between the causal arrow and other arrows such as the psychological arrow needs to be revisited.

Suppose as I suggested in the last section, determinists agree that there are no longer causes of the future. All causes obtained in the distant past, and causal chains are only an unraveling of an initial causal force like a ball of string that unravels from the beginning of time in the forward direction. The causal arrow is really an unraveling arrow from past to future. The string moves outward in a certain direction. The direction in which the string unravels is what we call the future.

This move solves the problem of inconsistency by turning the causal arrow into a trivial arrow. On the unraveling image, the entire future is implicit at the beginning of time. That is a coherent position, but if all events are on a par, that eliminates the causal arrow in the usual sense, and it appears to be committed to the position that the past and future are as real as the present. Notice also that it is inconsistent with the modal arrow, so if you are not already convinced that there is no modal arrow, then subscribing to the unraveling theory is another reason to give it up.

My conclusion is that if the causal arrow exists and there is a transfer principle for it, it is inconsistent with determinism.

The determinist can modify the causal arrow to an arrow of unravelability, but that involves commitment to a view of time that not all determinists want to accept. That need not be an objection, of course, but it reveals another way that our worries about fatalism hide the fact that there are more general problems in the logic and metaphysics of time.

Notice that my argument that the Consequence Argument for the incompatibility of determinism and free will is defective does not support compatibilism, and it is neutral on whether causal fatalism is true. My point is that a very well-known argument that determinism entails fatalism has the same problem I have identified in a series of previous arguments. There is an incoherence in the use of the causal arrow of time in fatalist arguments. Others have argued that determinism entails fatalism by a route that is intended to bypass the causal arrow.[5] My arguments in this book do not show that fatalism is false. What they intend to show is that well-known forms of argument for fatalism are fatally flawed.

It is common for philosophers to maintain that the causal arrow exists, but if we could travel backward in time, things would be different. So, let's change our point of view on the causal arrow and suppose that causal chains can operate in the backward direction. Given that physical laws are deterministic in both directions, that seems possible.[6] True, we do not think that way because we do not know how to explain earlier times by later times, whereas we have no trouble explaining later times by earlier times. We travel into the future automatically, but we do not know how to travel into the past. We know the past, not the future; we deliberate about the future, not the past. If the second law of thermodynamics is a law,

---

[5] A possible way to avoid the causal arrow is given by Ted Warfield (2000), who argues that the following proposition entails that determinism is incompatible with free will: For every x and S, if S is free to make it the case that x, then possibly x and the state of the world in the distant past and the laws of nature obtained. Warfield defends the truth of this proposition, and therefore, the incompatibility of determinism and free will.

[6] See Baron and Miller (2019), chap. 5 for a discussion of this point.

there is an asymmetry of entropy.[7] But our physical theories allow description of the fundamental processes of nature in a temporally reversed order. In fact, it is puzzling to explain temporal asymmetry and directionality in terms of laws that are symmetrical. Backward causation ought to be possible, given the laws of physics. Can the idea of backward causation escape our trilemmas and fatalist arguments?

Section 2. Backward causation and backward counterfactual power

2.1. Does backward agent causation exist?

In introducing the idea of the necessity of the past at the beginning of Part One, I mentioned an interpretation of it that is incoherent. That is the idea that we can *change* the past. Changing implies that there are two timelines—one before the change, and one after the change, where the second timeline supersedes the first. I assume that there is only one timeline, so changing the timeline is not at issue. Even if time is not a line, as I will propose in the final part of this book, changing the past is not possible.

A second interpretation of the necessity of the past was the topic of Part One. According to that interpretation, the past has a form of necessity that permits it to be analyzed in a way that is parallel to logical necessity. I argued that if the fatalist intends the necessity of the past to be temporally asymmetrical (the past has it, the future does not), then unless he intends his argument to be a *reductio*, he cannot use it as an implied premise in order to reject it in the argument for fatalism. I then argued that temporally asymmetrical necessity is inconsistent with the supposition that there are

---

[7] Baron and Miller (2019, 138–142) give a short discussion of the idea that the second law of thermodynamics is not a law of nature.

propositions about the past that entail propositions about the future. Propositions about God's past infallible beliefs, the past truth of propositions about the future, and the past history of the world when combined with causal determinism are in that category, but there are others. I concluded that the cost of preserving this notion of the necessity of the past is too high. We should reject it.

In the previous section of this Part, I discussed another interpretation of the necessity of the past—the metaphysical principle that the past is causally closed. I argued that that interpretation is inconsistent with the idea that the future is causable if there is a transfer of causability principle. It also generates trilemmas parallel to the trilemmas in Part One. In this section I want to examine the idea that there is backward causation as a possible way out of fatalist arguments and as a way to avoid the trilemmas I have discussed.

The notion of backward causation is radical but not obviously unintelligible. We think that time moves from causes to effects, but why not from effects to causes? Even if we accept the idea that time moves in the direction of increased entropy, and in the direction of what we remember to what we anticipate, do we have to accept the position that time has a causal arrow that goes from causes to effects? In the last section I showed ways that the causal arrow is muddled. If it is muddled anyway, maybe backward causation is not so radical an idea. It can be fun to consider the possibility that backward causation can get us out of the fatalist arguments. But if there is backward causation, what happens to the other arrows of time?

The possibility of backward causation should be distinguished from the possibility of time travel. Time travel requires a causal loop, whereas backward causation does not. When you get into your time machine, that causes you to emerge at an earlier time, and that leads to a causal sequence resulting in you going "back" to the future from where you started. In contrast, if a cause comes later in time than its effect, there is no reason why the earlier effect must be on a causal chain leading to the later cause. So backward causation need not lead to that particular puzzle.

One issue that comes up immediately in any discussion of causation influenced by David Hume (2000) is the problem of how to distinguish cause from effect. Hume argued that an account of causation based on empirically observable events distinguishes cause from effect solely by temporal order. Given two events that are constantly conjoined, the cause is identified as the one that is prior. But whatever the merit of Hume's analysis of event causation, it is much harder to make the case that the cause is whatever precedes the event with which it is conjoined if we are talking about agent causation. When you decide to pick up a cup of coffee and take a sip, your sense of causing the sipping is not due to temporal order. Admittedly, the idea of reverse agent causation jumbles our mind, but I want to turn to the clearest and most enjoyable paper I know of defending its possibility—Michael Dummett's (1964) paper, "Bringing About the Past."

Dummett argues that if backward intentional causation is impossible, we ought to be able to convince a person that it is impossible regardless of the empirical situation. So, he feels free to imagine a situation that is empirically favorable to the belief in backward causation and challenges us to figure out how we could convince a reasonable person that it is not possible. He imagines a native tribe that sends its young men out on a hunt every other year. They are gone for six days. It takes them two days to get to the hunting ground, they hunt for two days, and it takes them two days to return. Observers go with them to see whether they acquit themselves with bravery. While they are gone, the chief does a ritual dance during the entire six days they are gone with the purpose of helping them succeed. The chief believes that his dancing is causally operative in bringing about the bravery of the young men. You, the skeptic about backward causation, say to him, "Why dance the last two days? After four days the hunt is over. Either they were brave, or they were not. It's too late for your dance to have any effect." He replies, "Ha! Our last chief thought the way you do. He only danced four days, and you know what? It was disaster every time. After I became chief, I got sick twice after four days and had to stop dancing. Each time the hunt was unsuccessful. It is crucial that the dancing continue for six days."

Certain that you can convince him, you say, "But once they come back and you find out whether they have been successful, you would not continue dancing, would you?" "No, of course not," he replies, "but there is still a point in dancing when I do not yet know the report." Surprised, you realize that he believes that dancing in ignorance of the outcome is what is causally efficacious, so you say, "How can your knowledge have anything to do with it? I thought you believed that it is the dancing that does the trick."

Suppose that you convince him that his state of knowledge or ignorance has no effect on the young hunters' bravery. That allows you to challenge him to dance after the young men return and the report is that they were not brave. The chief accepts the challenge, but then finds himself unable to dance. One time a neighboring tribe attacks and he has to go out and fight them. Another time he gets an injury. Once he does dance, but since he does not believe that dancing is a 100 percent guarantee of bravery, he is not much bothered by it. Dummett then mentions another possible outcome. Sometimes the chief is told that the young men have not been brave, but he continues to dance, and then he finds out that he was misinformed. They were brave after all. That may lead him to cease trusting the reports of the observers independently of his decision to perform the dance.

Dummett draws an interesting conclusion from this story. He says that the chief started out with two beliefs:

(i) There is a positive correlation between his dancing and the previous brave behavior of the young men, and there is a positive correlation between his not dancing and the previous cowardly behavior of the young men.
(ii) Dancing was something in his power to do.

He can consistently hold on to these two beliefs provided he gives up another belief:

> (iii) It is always possible to find out what happened in the past independently of one's present intentions (348).

These three beliefs, Dummett concludes, are inconsistent.

Compare the situation of the dancing chief with the Newcomb puzzle. When you begin to play the game, you have two beliefs:

> (i) There is a positive correlation between the choice of one box and the previous act of the predictor of putting $1 million in the second box, and there is a positive correlation between the choice of two boxes and the previous act of the predictor of putting nothing in the second box.
>
> (ii) The choice of one or two boxes is in your power to do.

But what happens if the audience can see into the box, and they tell you what they see; or perhaps the box is torn, and you can peek into it yourself. What will you think? If we follow Dummett, we will say that you can continue to believe (i) and (ii) as long as you give up another highly reasonable belief:

> (iii) It is always possible to find out what is in the box independently of your present intention to choose one box or two.

Like the dancing chief, Dummett's argument would be that you can continue to believe in your power to decide only if you trust that power more than the report of the eyewitnesses or even your own perceptual ability when you peek into the box. The chief and the player in the Newcomb game can consistently believe in their causal influence over the past provided that they think that the past, like the future, is not something we can always know independently of knowing our own intentions regarding it.

Dummett's defense of the reasonableness of believing in backward agent causation has a big price. It means that the process of backward causation interferes with knowledge of past events, and in that way it jeopardizes the psychological arrow of time. But I am not sure that Dummett is right in claiming an incompatibility among (i), (ii), and (iii) anyway. If the chief is informed that the young men were not brave, he might disbelieve it, as Dummett allows, but he might believe it, in which case he could still believe (iii). In that case he would treat the information that the young men were not brave as also a discovery that either further dancing will not work in this case or that he will not continue dancing. If the latter, he will be disappointed in himself, not because he can't dance, but because he won't dance. He can consistently maintain that dancing is in his power and that it is positively correlated with past brave behavior. Further, he can maintain that the dancing causes the brave behavior, not the other way around. And he can treat the past as something that he can always in principle find out independently of his present intentions.

In the Newcomb puzzle, there is a 100 percent correlation between your decision and the contents of the boxes. Suppose that you are in that situation, and you find out that there is nothing in the second box before you decide how many boxes to take. Could you consistently believe the Newcomb version of (i)–(iii) above? It seems to me that you could. You would think that you *should* take one box, but you would be disappointed in yourself because finding out that there is nothing in the second box amounts to finding out that you will not choose one box. You would have to give up the idea that we cannot know our future choices before we make them.

However, there is an oddity in finding out that you won't choose one box, and the chief's finding out that he won't dance. The distinction between believing that we won't and believing that we can't is blurred. There is a psychological difficulty, perhaps impossibility, in doing deliberately what we already firmly believe we will do and in deliberately refraining from doing what we firmly believe we will not do. That explains why the chief might not want to find out whether the young men were brave until the end of the six days. He would not want to be informed that they were brave since that might psychologically hamper his ability to choose to dance. Similarly, if he is informed that they were not brave, that amounts to finding out that he will not dance, and that would make it difficult for him to go through the process of decision-making. For human beings, deliberating about a decision must be made in ignorance of the outcome. If you know in advance what you will choose, how can you deliberate? But that is a feature of human psychology, not a metaphysical law about agent causation.

I conclude that backward agent causation can be consistently maintained if we give up an aspect of the psychological arrow of time. We think that deliberation comes before knowledge of our future, but it does not come before knowledge of the past. We remember the past or find out about it from others; we deliberate about the future and cannot find out about it from others. In the story of the dancing chief and in the Newcomb puzzle, backward causation is coherent provided that it is also coherent that we can find out something about the past that tells us our future choice before we make it. But there is a psychological obstacle in finding out a future choice before we make it, which means that when we make the choice, it is not a choice in the usual sense. I think that that is why it is important in the gospel story of Peter's denial of Christ that he forgets the prophecy at the time of the denial. If he is ignorant of his future choice, he can make it in the usual way. But if he knows what he will do, he is psychologically hindered from choosing. I think, then, that backward agent causation has the same psychological problem as self-foreknowledge. Possibly there is a causal law about the conditions for making choices that would be violated in the case of self-foreknowledge. If so, self-foreknowledge of a deliberate choice is causally impossible and backward agent causation is causally impossible, not because causes have to precede effects, but because backward agent causation permits the possibility of self-foreknowledge, and that is causally impossible. It is the psychology of choosing that is the problem, not the order of causation.

An old argument against backward agent causation is the Bilking argument, which comes from Max Black (1956). The objection is that whenever an event B has occurred, it is possible, in principle, to intervene in the course of events and prohibit the alleged cause A from occurring. If so, A cannot be the cause of B. Let's take the dancing chief as our example. If the hunt has already occurred, and you find out that the young tribesmen were courageous, it is always possible to prevent the chief from dancing the last two days. All you have to do is injure him or tell him about an urgent event that gives him a reason to stop dancing. Similarly, once the game host puts the money in the boxes, a member of the audience can intervene before you make a decision, and they can cause you to choose whatever they want.

I do not think that this objection works. Think about the relation between cause and effect in the forward direction. You accidentally push a glass toward the edge of a table, and before it falls, it is possible that your companion catches it and prevents it from falling, but we can suppose that she does not or there is no companion to stop it. Your action is the cause and the falling glass is the effect even though there are other possible worlds in which there is an intervention. In parallel fashion, if the young men are brave, there will be no intervention before the chief dances the whole six days, but there could have been in some alternate world, in which case the young men would turn out not to have been brave. In the Newcomb puzzle, the fact that the game host puts $1 million in the second box means that there will be no intervention before you make your choice of one box, but there are alternate worlds in which there is an intervention, and in those worlds there is no $1 million in the second box.

But the Bilking defender will insist that intervention can still happen *in this world*, the world in which the effect has already happened. But do we know that? Have we tried it? Like Dummett's chief, we might find that when we try, the world does not cooperate with our plans. Dummett imagines that you challenge the chief to dance when the report is that they were cowardly, and he finds that he is unable to dance. So, you might try to intervene once you know that the effect has occurred, and you find that you are unable to do so. Or maybe you do intervene, and that is an exception to the general causal connection between the dancing and the past bravery, or the player's decision and the past action of the game host. Maybe every time you attempt to intervene, you are not able to, or it does not work as intended. Even more likely, you intervene and find out that the alleged effect did not happen after all. When you intervene and prevent something that otherwise would happen in the future, you make it not happen. When you intervene and prevent something that otherwise would have happened in the past, you make it not have happened. If you successfully intervene, it did not happen, just as when you successfully intervene in an event that is about to happen, it does not happen. It is possible that the process of intervention is the same for both past and future.

Let us go back to divine foreknowledge. Suppose I am right that divine knowledge is not caused by its object. God foreknows that on a certain day Susan will pray that she will get tenure, and God "responds" to the prayer before it happens. That has the same psychological problem as backward agent causation for reasons parallel to the dancing chief. If Susan is informed via letter that she got tenure and she believes it, it is psychologically impossible for her to pray a petitionary prayer that she got tenure. If she is informed that she was denied tenure, her prayer also will not be petitionary. She can pray that there was a mistake, but then she is doubting the information contained in the letter, like the chief doubting the report of the observers. So, one of the reasons she may hesitate before reading the letter is that she knows her causal influence over the event is closed once she is informed of its contents. But that is because of the causal structure of human psychology, not because of the impossibility of backward causation. What is psychologically but not metaphysically impossible is petitionary prayer over the past while knowing the past outcome, and that is the same as the psychological problem of making a choice while knowing what choice we will make. There might be exceptions to the usual past-to-future causal arrow, and if so, there would be exceptions to the psychological arrow.

What are the implications for fatalism? Notice that the possibility of backward causation does not in itself escape fatalism. It is possible that every event is fated by other events even if some of those events are in the future. Maybe there is no causal arrow, and all events are equally determined, some by events in their past, and some by events in their future. But in the case of divine foreknowledge, if there is a causal relation between our act and God's foreknowledge of it, backward causation opens up the possibility that God's foreknowledge is causally determined by our act, thereby preserving our free will.

There is one point I would like to make before leaving it aside. It is interesting that the anomalies in backward causation and the psychological arrow do not apply to God. I assume that God does not deliberate before making a future choice. In fact, it is unlikely that God ever deliberates, and he does not remember the past in a way that is different from his knowing the future. There is no psychological arrow for God. Presumably, that is true whether or not God is in time. For God, every choice was made before time was created, and the effects of the choice unfold at the proper time.[8] So, there is no problem of divine self-foreknowledge parallel to the problem of human self-foreknowledge. But the reason the possibility of backward agent causation is exciting to some anti-fatalists is that it can be used as a way out of the dilemma of divine foreknowledge

---

[8] For those who believe that God does deliberate and choose in time, divine self-foreknowledge is an issue to be resolved, but I will not discuss it since it does not affect the argument of this book.

and human free will. Your action causes God to have foreknowledge of it.

George Mavrodes (1984) proposes in his paper on preventing the past that the coronation of Queen Elizabeth II in 1953 could even now (in 1983) be preventable. He agrees that if she was in fact crowned, then it *will not* be prevented, but it does not follow that it *cannot* be prevented, a point I made in discussing the dancing chief. We might prevent events in the past all the time, and how would we know that, given that there is no way to compare the actual chain of events in the past with alternative chains, just as we cannot compare the actual chain of events in the future with alternative chains? Compare the fact that if Prince William is crowned at some time in the future, then it will not be prevented, but we would not say that it cannot be prevented. Mavrodes proposes that we cause past events all the time. That is when we cause God to have beliefs in the past about what we are doing.

A recent argument that our actions cause God's past beliefs comes from Ryan Wasserman (2021). Wasserman suggests that the way in which we cause God's past beliefs is similar to what we find in time travel stories, only God is less a time traveler than a time viewer (21). Wasserman argues that the causal dependence of God's knowledge on our acts avoids problems in interpreting the dependence as modal, counterfactual, or metaphysical dependence, and it gives a plausible story about how God knows the future, thereby supporting an anti-fatalist conclusion.

I have said that I think it is unlikely that the relation between our acts and God's beliefs is causal, but let us suppose that Mavrodes and Wasserman are right. Is there any incoherence in their proposals? One reason that backward causation is very hard to imagine is that we have no trouble seeing how past events explain future events but not the reverse. This is a point made by Dummett early in his 1964 paper. He writes:

If we imagine ourselves as intelligent trees observing such a world [of reverse causation] ... it is clear that we should have great difficulty in arriving at causal explanations that account for events in terms of the processes which *led up to* them. The sapling grows gradually smaller, finally reducing itself to an apple pip; then an apple is gradually constituted around the pip from ingredients found in the soil; at a certain moment the apple rolls along the ground, gradually gaining momentum, bounces a few times, and then suddenly takes off vertically and attaches itself with a snap to the bough of an apple tree. Viewed from the standpoint of gross observation, this process contains many totally unpredictable elements. (334)

Notice that if a cause explains the effect, and a cause occurs after its effect, all explanations in a backward causation situation would have to be from some subsequent moment. We would have to wait for the causal explanation to occur. Maybe we can accept that, but it would be very troubling. A world of backward causation is not a world for impatient people.

I have argued that the so-called necessity of the past leads to trilemmas. The trilemma of Part One arises from the idea of accidental necessity. The trilemmas of section 1 of this part arise from causal closure. Let's look at what the hypothesis of backward causation does to the causal trilemmas.

Recall that the first trilemma arises from the inconsistency of the following:

(1) A causal arrow from past to future
(2) The transfer of Non-causability Principle
(3) The determinist thesis

The second trilemma is the same except that it substitutes rule Beta for (2) above.

If backward causation is possible, we can accept (2) and (3) by denying (1). Neither (2) nor (3) explicitly refers to the order of causation, nor does rule Beta, but (3) would need to be reinterpreted if it is defined in the most common way. Typically, determinism is understood to be the thesis that every event is necessitated by *prior* events when conjoined with the laws of nature. Interpreted that way, backward causation requires the denial of (3) as well as (1). But determinism can be redefined as the thesis that every event is necessitated by some other events when conjoined with the laws of nature, leaving open the issue of when the necessitating events occur and whether there are causal loops. With this interpretation, determinism loses much of its predictive power, but it is a way out of the trilemmas of the last section.

Backward causation probably has metaphysical commitments that I will not discuss. I am leaving backward causation open as a possibility, but I am not endorsing it. One of my purposes is to unsettle our intuitions about arrows of time. The possibility of backward causation does that.

2.2. Counterfactual power over the past

We have examined three interpretations of the necessity of the past and found them wanting. The first was the idea that the past cannot be changed. That one is trivial and can be dismissed quickly. Second, we examined the idea that the past is necessary in the sense intended by Ockham and parallel to logical necessity. That was the topic of Part One. I argued that that idea leads to a trilemma, and unless we want to deny that there are any propositions about the past that entail propositions about the future, the outcome of that discussion is that the necessity of the past in this sense must be rejected also. Third, we examined the idea that the necessity of the past is the causal closure of the past. I have argued that that idea cannot be consistently used by the fatalist unless she is willing to deny that there are causes of the future. In addition, the causal closure of the past leads to trilemmas parallel to the trilemma of Part One. There are ways out of those trilemmas that deny the causal arrow. One possibility is that determinism is true but includes both backward and forward causation. Another possibility is that determinism is false and backward causation explains the relationship between a free act and previous infallible foreknowledge of it. But if backward causation is possible, there are puzzles in the relationship between backward agent causation and the psychological arrow of human knowledge that would need further examination.

In this section I will investigate a fourth interpretation of the necessity of the past, a principle that John Martin Fischer (1983) has called the "Fixed Past Constraint." That is the principle that there is nothing I can do now which is such that if I were to do it, the past would have been different from what it was.[9] This principle does not explicitly refer to causation. Instead, it denies that there is counterfactual power over the past, a power that might or might not be causal. Fischer (1983) uses his counterfactual version of the fixity of the past to argue that divine foreknowledge entails the fixity of the future.[10] The argument is parallel to the other fatalist arguments in this book.

We have already encountered related counterfactual claims in earlier sections of this part of the book. I mentioned in section 1.2 that Van Inwagen (2000) proposed a counterfactual analysis of his rule Beta to avoid objections. His proposal is to alter the N operator to the following: Np = p and no one can or ever could do anything such that if she did it, it might be false that p. The principle

---

[9] In the introduction to a collection of papers on foreknowledge, Fischer (1989) refines this principle and calls it the Principle of the Fixity of the Past: For any action Y, agent S, and time T, if it is true that if S were to do Y at T, then some hard fact about the past (relative to T) would not have been a fact, then S cannot do X at T.
[10] Fischer (1984) replies to proposed counterexamples to the Fixed Past Principle in addition to giving his basic argument for the incompatibility of divine foreknowledge and human free will. See also Fischer (2011a) for his more recent use of the counterfactual version of the necessity of the past and his response to objections.

can then be applied to the distant history of the world and causal laws. Michael Dummett uses the term "bringing about" rather than "causing" in his paper about agent power over the past, and that leaves open the possibility that his story about the dancing chief is a story of counterfactual power over the past rather than backward causation. If so, the question would be whether there is anything the chief can do now which is such that were he to do it, the past would have been different from what it was.

To make matters even more complicated, sometimes the causal relation itself is given a counterfactual analysis. In this section I will proceed without assuming that counterfactual power is a causal process but without ruling that out either. This approach is attractive when the issue is the relationship between your act and states of God, which are probably outside the realm of causation, as I have said. So even if you do not *cause* God's past beliefs, we can ask if it is possible that you can act in such a way that if you did such an act, God's past beliefs would have been different. If so, Fischer's Fixed Past Principle is false as applied to God and it does not lead to theological fatalism.

The claim that there is counterfactual power over the past was influentially argued by Alvin Plantinga (1986), who attributed it to Ockham. If it works, it is a way of getting to the conclusion that God's past beliefs are not accidentally necessary without going through an account of the difference between hard facts and soft facts about the past. Plantinga's intention is to define accidental necessity and contingency directly in terms of human power rather than via an account of the difference between past and future. His approach detaches the idea of accidental necessity and contingency from the arrow of time.

Plantinga denies the Fixed Past Constraint (FPC) without distinguishing that part of the past to which FPC applies (the accidentally necessary) from that part of it to which it does not apply. As far as I can tell, he does not have an argument for denying FPC, and he seems to leave open the possibility that nothing in the past is accidentally necessary in Ockham's sense. I think Plantinga is right that FPC is on weaker ground than the denial of backward causation. Still, Fischer claims that it is true, and Plantinga claims that it is false. Fischer relies upon intuitions. Plantinga argues that we can imagine that those intuitions are wrong. What are we to make of that dispute?

Let us look first at how the lack of counterfactual power over the past can be used in a fatalist argument. The transfer of counterfactual power principle would go as follows:

Transfer of Counterfactual Power Principle

> If there is nothing I can do now which is such that if I did it, some event E in the past would have been different from what it was, and if necessarily, if E occurs then F will occur, then there is nothing I can do now which is such that if I did it, F would be different from what it will be.

This principle says that there is no counterfactual power over anything in the future entailed by something in the past over which we lack counterfactual power. Given the FPC, we have no counterfactual power over anything that occurred in the past, and by the Transfer of Counterfactual Power Principle, we have no counterfactual power over anything in the future entailed by anything in the past. If there is something in the past that entails the entire future, we have no counterfactual power over anything in the future.

There is no counterfactual arrow of time. We get the same conclusion we got with the other interpretations of the necessity of the past. If FPC is intended to reflect an arrow of time, it fails as long as there are propositions about the past that entail propositions about the future.

Let's look now at how Plantinga's use of counterfactual power can help the anti-fatalist. His claim that there is counterfactual power over the past is not as unsettling as the claim that there is backward causation because a counterfactual arrow of time is not as fixed in science, philosophy, and ordinary thinking as the causal arrow. Counterfactual power did not make a sustained appearance in philosophy until less than fifty years ago with the analysis of counterfactuals, and most people probably have not thought about it at all. But the idea of counterfactual power is appealing when a causal connection is not relevant, as is probably the case with the relationship between God's knowledge and our acts.

I think that Plantinga was right that we know of nothing that rules out the truth of a proposition like *I can paint my house yellow, and if I decided to do so, God would have known that I would a very long time ago.* But defending the possible truth of that proposition requires a logical and metaphysical story that explains it. I suspect that the explanation would focus on the "because" relation. God foreknows my act *because* I am going to do it, where "because" does not have a causal sense. What kind of *because* would that be? There are counterfactual accounts of the "because" relation, but, clearly, they are unhelpful if we want to use the "because" relation to explain how certain counterfactuals can be true. When we are referring to agents with intelligence and intentions, we say that they act in certain ways for reasons. It is natural to use the term "because" when referring to those reasons. "I went to the café because I was hungry," "I told him the time of the meeting because he asked." "Because" is also sometimes appropriate when referring to an emotional state: "I gave the panhandler some change because I felt sorry for her." Some reasons can be universalized to any rational being and are predictable for that reason: "He knows that he will die because he knows that all humans die." That is based on a purely cognitive operation where preferences and feelings are irrelevant. Other "because" sentences are individual and personal and cannot be predicted because they are not based on causal laws. The example of giving to the panhandler is probably in that category. If God has personal reasons for acting and has foreknowledge, the following could be true: "You can pray, and if you prayed, God would have responded to the prayer in advance, and depending upon God's reasons for acting, the past might have been different."

In the dancing chief story, I argued that consistency would not force the chief to give up his belief in the independent knowledge of the past because he can interpret the news that the young men were not brave as the news that he will not dance, not that he cannot dance, and he undoubtedly will be disappointed in himself. Suppose now that we are not considering backward causation but backward counterfactual power. Would that change the story? We can imagine that the chief does not have a theory of backward causation. Instead, he thinks that his future dancing is such that it corresponds to the young men's past behavior, but without any theory about the nature of the connection. He might think that the connection is mysterious, and he might not care. He might say that he has no idea what the mechanism is that links his dancing with the behavior of the young men. All he cares about is that the correlation between his behavior and the young tribesmen's past behavior gives him a reason to dance. If he does not dance, he believes that he could have danced, and if he had done so, the outcome would have been different. It does not matter if the outcome is something that has already happened.

Suppose now that his tribal scientists tell him that the idea that he has counterfactual power over the past behavior of the young hunters violates natural laws. They have found no other example of backward power, and they have tried many times to find it. Natural laws are universal, they say. If there is a counterfactual relation between event A and event B, then there is a counterfactual relation between events like A and events like B, but they know of no instances of events like dancing or any other intentional act that are related to past events in the required way. They conclude that even if the chief has counterfactual power over the future, he does not have counterfactual power over the past. But let's suppose also that the religious leaders of the tribe say that they know of many instances in which praying about something that already happened, when offered in a state of humble supplication to the gods, had a favorable outcome. They say that knowing the outcome before praying prevents the prayer from having the attitude the gods appreciate—making a request in a state of humility. That is why prayer does not work after the petitioner finds out the result. It will not be the right kind of prayer. They tell the chief that his dance is a prayer. If he finds out the result before he completes the entire six-day dance, he will be sorry that he is no longer able to complete the prayer for reasons pertaining to his own psychology. If he can get himself to forget what he learns, he can still perform the dance and it can still work. When told that the tribe's scientists say that there cannot be such a backward relation, they are unmoved. "We did not maintain that the prayer works by natural laws. The gods can see into the future and decide how to respond."

With this advice from his religious counselors, I can see why the chief can reasonably hold on to his belief that there is something he can do now, namely a ritual dance, that entreats the gods to look favorably on the young hunters and assure their past bravery. He can believe that his scientists are right about natural causal events, and his priests are right about a non-causal counterfactual power over the past. He can continue to believe that he can find out what happened in the past independently of his decision to dance, but he will conclude that dancing in ignorance of the outcome is necessary, not because ignorance has some special power, but because petitionary prayer is what works, and a petition is not a petition when made in knowledge of whether the prayer is successful.

Let's return to the counterfactual arrow of time. I have suggested that the causal arrow is intimately tied to the way we think of time; the counterfactual arrow is not. Denying the causal arrow upsets the way we think of physical processes; denying the counterfactual arrow does not upset anything in our understanding of the physical world if the counterfactual power goes through a deity whose reasons to act are not causes. That gives the Plantinga-style Ockhamist an opening to say that there can be counterfactual power that is not connected to a past/future difference in the truth of the relevant counterfactual propositions. Maybe there is causal power over the past, but counterfactual power is more plausible than causal power, and it is the natural interpretation of the relation between God's knowledge and our acts if that relation is not causal.

I think that the Ockham/Plantinga move is the best way to escape the argument for theological fatalism, provided that counterfactual power can be separated from causal power, but my arguments in this book show that that is not the end of the matter. The failure of the arguments from the necessity of the past and the causal closure of the past disrupts our understanding of the nature of time. If there are propositions about the past that entail propositions about the future, there is no modal arrow of time, no causal arrow of time, and no counterfactual arrow of time. The fatalist argues that there is no arrow because the future is like the past. I have argued that the arrows do not exist because of the trilemmas I have described. If Plantinga is right, the counterfactual arrow fails for a different reason. It fails because the past, or an important part of it, is like the future, not because the future is like the past. The failure of these arrows means that we need a metaphysical account of movement and change to supplant the intuitive Aristotelian idea of potency and act. Without the arrows, the ancient problem of change becomes harder, and problems in explaining the nature of change affect other philosophical issues such as human deliberation and action. If counterfactual power over God's past beliefs saves our free will and permits us to avoid the trilemmas of the modal arrow and the causal arrow, we are still left with the problem that the collapse of the arrows has ramifications for an enormous range of philosophical issues.

We can reject all the temporal arrows we have discussed—the modal arrow, the causal arrow, and the counterfactual arrow, but that forces us to disconnect all of those arrows from the psychological arrow. Is the psychological arrow of time an arrow of the same thing as the modal or causal or counterfactual arrow? If the latter arrows do not exist, where does that leave the psychological arrow? What is it an arrow *of*? Fracturing one or more arrows fractures our sense of what time is. Of course, all our problems can be solved if no proposition about the past entails a proposition about the future. We can save our sense of time by radically limiting our metaphysical, scientific, and theological hypotheses. But would we really want to do that? You decide.

Section 3. Conclusion to Parts One and Two

In Part One of this book, I argued that a standard argument for theological fatalism can be unpacked in three steps to reveal a problem in the logic of time that has nothing to do with fatalism. The problem centers on the modal arrow of time when combined with a thesis about the past that entails a thesis about the future. My solution to the problem is to reject the modal arrow. That means that any argument for fatalism that uses such an arrow should be rejected. As I have said, it does not follow that fatalism is false, but fatalists have a much narrower range of options in defending fatalism if I am right.

In Part Two I proposed parallel problems for the causal arrow of time. The well-known consequence argument that determinism entails fatalism has defects that should lead us to reject it. But again, we cannot conclude that determinism does not entail fatalism. But if it does, it is through a different route than one that requires the premise of a causal arrow that is at best muddled and probably incoherent. I believe that fatalism is false, but my purpose in this book is not to attack fatalism; rather, it is to attack a series of standard arguments for it. My aim is twofold: To significantly narrow the range of possibly successful fatalist arguments, and more importantly, to show how fatalist arguments reveal deep confusions in our views about time.

I began this book with three common fatalist arguments that have the same structure and depend upon the same key assumptions—the necessity of the past, and a transfer of necessity principle. Each one begins with a different premise that people accept or reject for different reasons, but since the structure of the arguments is the same, I conjectured that the differences among them are not deep. That might lead us to wonder whether once we are past the first premise, they stand or fall together. This is an interesting question because not only are the arguments usually treated separately, but it is also not uncommon for theists who are compatibilists about divine foreknowledge and human free will to be incompatibilists about determinism and free will in response to structurally identical arguments. One way they can do that is to accept one of the theistic solutions to theological fatalism, which separates the theological argument from the causal argument. They would then need to evaluate the other arguments of Part One, including the generalized argument that infallible foreknowledge entails fatalism. In Part One I argued for two main theses. One is that all the standard fatalist arguments from accidental necessity presuppose the modal arrow at the outset in order to deny the arrow, in which case there is an inconsistency lurking in the argument, made explicit in section 2.2. That led to my second thesis, which is that the assumption of the modal arrow and the Transfer of Accidental Necessity Principle is inconsistent with the truth of any proposition about the past that entails a proposition about the future, argued in section 2.3. I believe that the theist who accepts the entailment between divine foreknowledge and future human acts should conclude that the modal arrow is incoherent. It is not necessary to fall back on the well-known distinctively theistic responses to theological fatalism.

What should theists say about the causal arrow? They might think that the argument from the causal closure of the past succeeds in showing that determinism entails fatalism, but they would need to evaluate the arguments about causal closure in this part of the book as well as the arguments that are parallel to the arguments in Part One. The argument for causal fatalism from the causal closure of the past implicitly uses the causal arrow in order to deny it, and the causal arrow, like the modal arrow, has a generalized trilemma. Furthermore, can we say that the causal unpreventability of the past leads to fatalism when the uncausability of the past leads to the conclusion that there are no causes of the future? The causal arrow is in trouble. Rather than attack determinism directly, I think that it makes more sense for the theist to question the causal arrow.

What about the arguments for logical fatalism? As I mentioned earlier, those arguments have not received nearly as much attention as the other fatalist arguments. I have always thought that the position of Ockham that truth and necessity must be distinguished is the right answer. Unchangeable truth does not entail the necessity of the truth. But I realize that people who disagree about that often attempt to avoid the logical fatalist conclusion by denying that there are true future contingent propositions. I argued earlier that they must also deny the relation of entailment or identity between a proposition expressed in the future tense and a proposition about the same event in the present or past tense. Suppose that they do that. They could then apply the same move to escape theological fatalism. An infallible God does not know a future contingent truth because there isn't one, and they would also have to say that God's past infallible beliefs do not entail the truth of a proposition about a future event. Of course, anyone who is willing to deny that there are any propositions about the past that entail propositions about the future can escape all the arguments we have discussed, both the fatalist arguments and the trilemmas of time. That solution is still an open possibility.

The timelessness solution to theological fatalism is popular. Elsewhere (Zagzebski 2011) I have argued that it is inadequate, but suppose that it works. It could also be used as a way out of logical fatalism since it is plausible that propositions are timeless entities that do not have truth value at times. That move would not work against causal fatalism, and it can explain why a theist might accept the fatalist consequences of determinism but not the fatalist consequences of future truth and divine foreknowledge.

The literature on causal fatalism usually focuses on the analysis of free will and the Principle of Alternate Possibilities (PAP). If PAP is false, and I have argued that it is (Zagzebski 1991, chap. 6), that move could work against all the fatalist arguments that use PAP. It would not touch the arguments in Part One and Part Two that do not refer to free will, and that is why I believe that discussion of PAP in the context of fatalist arguments misses an underlying problem.

How does Ockhamism in either the hard fact/soft fact version or the counterfactual power version work against all these arguments? As I argued in Part One, if every proposition about the past that entails a proposition about the future is in the soft past, as was proposed in early formulations of Ockhamism, then all the fatalist arguments are escaped by removing the starting propositions from the real or hard past. The past truth of propositions about the future is in the soft past; God's past foreknowledge is in the soft past. If determinism is true, the entire past history of the world in conjunction with the laws of nature is in the soft past. The inconsistency between accidental necessity/contingency and the entailment between any proposition about the past and a proposition about the future is resolved by the position that all such past propositions are in the soft past. As I mentioned, Ockhamists have recognized that the entailment relation between past and future will not work as a way to distinguish the hard past from the soft past, but if it could be made to work, it could save the compatibility of divine foreknowledge and human free will. But the Ockhamist would have to say that if determinism is true, there is no such thing as the hard past because the conjunction of all propositions about the past, given causal laws, entails the entire future. That gives the Ockhamist a very strong reason to reject determinism apart from free will.

I have said that the counterfactual power version of Ockhamism might be a successful move against theological fatalism. It could also be used against the argument for logical fatalism. Can it be used against causal fatalism? That is trickier. You might, like Plantinga, accept the idea that there is something you will not do, but if you were to do it, God would have foreknown that you would do it, in which case the past would have been different. For the same reason, it might be natural to say also that there is something you can do now which you won't do, but if you did, a proposition that was false in the past would have been true. Can you also say that there is something you can do now which is such that if you did it, some natural event in the past that does not involve divine foreknowledge would have been different? Perhaps. David Lewis (1981) refers to "local miracles" involving violation of the laws. If we use a weak Humean view of natural laws that construes them as true generalizations, that could permit the possibility that an agent in a deterministic world is able to do otherwise, and if she did so, a law describing her choice would be different.[11] Plantinga does not mention this use of his counterfactual Ockhamist approach, but if it succeeds, it could be used as a reply to all three fatalist arguments.

We have seen that the dancing chief and the Newcomb puzzle reveal anomalies in the psychological arrow of time. The chief might find out whether the young hunters were brave before he finishes his six-day dance, and you, the participant in the Newcomb game, might be able to peek into a torn box to see what is inside before you make your choice. If that means that you find out what you will choose before you choose it, and the chief finds out whether he will dance before he does it, it is possible to find out our future intention before we make it. That violates a feature of the psychological arrow of time because we take for granted that we can find out the past independently of our intentions, but we cannot find out our future intentions before we make them. This is a puzzle for both the psychological arrow and the causal arrow. It is also an example of how the arrows are connected.

---

[11] See John Perry (2004) for a discussion of this idea.

All the temporal arrows presuppose that time is linear and directional. Time moves from past to future. We can describe that direction in more than one way, but if the different ways we describe the direction do not coincide, that suggests we are very unclear about what it is that has the direction, and whether it is real. Fatalism is emotionally disturbing. The nature of time is not, although perhaps it should be. The genius of fatalist arguments is the way they explode our ideas about time and its arrows. We like to speak of time in metaphors of lines and arrows, but I think that the confusions uncovered in this book should lead us to rethink our metaphors. I will conclude with some conjectures on the arrow of time.

Part Three
Does Time Have an Arrow?

The existence of entailment relations between past and future shatters three arrows of time: the modal arrow, the causal arrow, and the counterfactual arrow. Of course, each of these arrows has been attacked in fatalist arguments, but those arguments make a confused use of the premise that the arrow exists in the attempt to deny it. I have argued that the arrows collapse for reasons that are independent of fatalism. If this was a different book, I might explore the problem from the other direction—the nature of entailment and our interest in preserving past-future entailments. But given that some of time's arrows are collapsing, I think that we should ask ourselves why we are so sure that time has any arrow at all. Do we even know that time is linear? Why do we use spatial images of lines and arrows when we imagine time?

The psychological arrow has survived the investigation of this book so far, but we need to look at it more closely because the experience of time is not necessarily the experience of an arrow. I think that the best defense of any of the temporal arrows is that they arise out of the way we experience time. That experience precedes every concept of a temporal arrow we have devised. In discussing the dancing chief, I said that the contrast between our access to the past and our access to the future would need to be modified if there is backward causation. The possibility of backward causation shakes the psychological arrow. For many people, that is reason enough to reject backward causation, but it might mean that we are not clear about what the experience of time commits us to.

Human consciousness moves in a sequence of before and after. That idea is nonnegotiable as far as I can see. I have argued that the modal, causal, and counterfactual arrows are broken, but the before-and-after sequence of human conscious experience cannot be broken. But where is the arrow? Does our experience force us to think that the sequence has a direction?

Many decades ago, Peter Strawson (1959, 62) imagined a world with time but no space. In support of his thought experiment, he mentioned Kant's position that space and time are two forms of sensibility. Kant said that time is the condition for all appearances whatever. Space is the condition for only outer appearances (Kant 1965, A34). The fact that physical science tells us that space and time are connected in a four-dimensional structure does not threaten Kant's point or Strawson's. Strawson proposes that it can be illuminating to imagine a world of time and no space, and then see what consequences follow (1959, 63). The world he imagines consists only of sounds.

A world of nothing but sounds seems metaphysically possible, and it intrigues me for different reasons than those that interested Strawson. My interest is in whether such a world would have arrows of time, and if so, what arrows it would have. A world consisting of nothing but time is not necessarily a world of only sounds, but a world of pure sound would be a world of pure time, and I propose that reflection on that world can help us identify the necessary features of the psychological arrow of time once we introduce a hearer.

Strawson admits that we can often assign spatial location to the source of a sound on the basis of the sound alone. A sound seems to come from the right or the left, from nearer or farther. But these features of a sound are not intrinsic to it, and they do not show that there cannot be a world of time and no space (1959, 65). We are able to make spatial inferences about sounds because we associate them with previous spatial experience. We can correlate our auditory experience with our non-auditory experience. Without non-auditory experience, we experience sounds as purely temporal. I think Strawson is right about that.

If the nature of time is what time would be with no mind experiencing it, imagining a world of nothing but sounds is the best way I know of to do it. Berkeley's famous argument that we cannot imagine any perceptual object without a perceiver was also famously mistaken. When I imagine a world of pure sound, I am not imagining a world of somebody hearing the sound. Imagining a world of sound with no hearers and no imaginers in it is not difficult. Still, we get the idea of time from our experience, so if we want to investigate the psychological arrow, we will need to add a hearer to our world of pure sound to see what the experience of nothing but sound would be like.

Kant claimed that all our experience presupposes the idea of time (1965, A31). He describes it as the a priori intuition of *one after another* (B49). I am not sure that Kant did not go too far in saying that it must be a world of one after another since that might suggest that the one before and the one after are distinguishable. What cannot be given up is that sound requires duration, and if so, duration is the essential ingredient of time. A musical note might be sustained and not be separated into one after another, but it must have duration. It moves from before to after even if there is no individual instant before and no individual instant after.

Let us go back to a world of pure sound before a hearer is introduced. Would time in that world have to be linear and directional? If what is intrinsic to time is that there is a before and after, possibly without a break as in a sustained chord, there is no reason to think that time must have a direction. When we think of direction, we use spatial terms—right, left, up, down—but a piece of music has no direction, even in our spatial world. We experience it as moving from before to after, but after is not a direction.

Must time in a world of pure sound be linear? When people speak of the linearity of time, they usually do so by contrasting linear time with cyclical time, but cyclical time is also linear. It is a line that goes in a circle. Linear time could move in a straight line, or in a circular line, or it could zigzag, or have many other patterns.

A world of pure sound need not be linear in any of these ways. It is true that when we speak of before and after, of one after another, we think of a line that can be enumerated t1, t2, t3, and so on; and it is common in philosophical discourse to pretend that we can count moments of time. We do that even though we know that time might be a continuum not divisible into countable moments. But even if time has moments that are countable, it does not follow that time has a linear form. We can count lots of things that are not linear—jellybeans in a jar, the names of the U.S. state capitals, the rules of the road. Time is sequential in that there is a sequence of before and after, so if sequences are linear by definition, time is linear in a trivial sense. To say that it is linear is to say nothing more than that it is sequence of before and after. The spatial metaphor of a line is not necessary. A world of pure sound is a world of one after another that is not linear, and it has no direction. Time need not have any kind of shape, and it need not be going anywhere. Linearity and direction are missing in our imaginary world of pure sounds.

Once we introduce ourselves into the world of pure sound, we introduce what we call a psychological arrow, but that is misleading. When we imagine experiencing pure sound with us in it, we imagine remembering earlier sounds and perhaps anticipating future sounds, as we often do when we are listening to a familiar piece of music. We experience a before and an after. But is there anything in the way we experience sound that makes it linear or directional? It is true that we use a common linear image when we distinguish a "short" time from a "long" time. The interval between one moment of time and another can be short or long. We call it a long time when one moment is separated from another by many other moments. We call it short when there are few in between. We imagine the difference between a short duration of time and a long duration of time as the difference between a short line and a long line. That image is natural, but it is not compelled by our experience of time. When listening to a piece of music, we experience the piece as having a short duration or a long duration. But as I have said, duration need not be linear in form. Even if we count the moments while we are listening to the music, what we are counting need not be linear, and it need not have a direction. Sound does not have to go anywhere, and the experience of sound does not take us anywhere.

I have proposed that the defense of the other temporal arrows would be their connection to the psychological arrow, but to be more accurate, it is the experience of before and after. As we hear the music, we think that what we have heard is over. What came before is fixed and untouchable. We have already experienced it, or we could have already experienced it. If we like, we can call it necessary or closed. What comes after is not fixed because it has not yet been experienced by anybody, or, at least, that is what we assume; and its causes might not yet have occurred, so we cannot predict what we will experience in the future. If we like, we call it contingent or open. That means that both the modal arrow and the causal arrow arise from the relation of before and after. The counterfactual arrow might also arise from temporal experience, but it is an arrow that explicitly refers to other possible worlds, and we do not have experience of other possible worlds. That makes the counterfactual arrow more puzzling than the other arrows, and it is easier to reject.

Insofar as physics is based on human observation, the arrows of physics we have devised also depend upon the sequential experience of before and after. We cannot give up the order of human experience, although we can give up our physical theories. However, that does not mean that the psychological experience of before and after is more basic in nature than the arrows of physics. Stephen Hawking (1988) argues that the thermodynamic arrow explains the psychological arrow. The direction of time in which we remember the past is the direction in which disorder increases. If the universe began in a disordered state, he says, disorder would decrease with time. We would see broken cups gathering together and jumping onto the table. Hawking maintains that in such a world our psychological arrow would also reverse. That is because there are many more disordered states than ordered ones, and the human mind "remembers" the small set of ordered states, which would mean that we would remember events in the future if the thermodynamic arrow was reversed. If the cup was first in pieces on the floor and then an unbroken cup on the table, we would "remember" the whole cup on the table when it was future. Our sense of the direction of time, he claims, is determined by the thermodynamic arrow. That makes the thermodynamic arrow almost trivial because we measure time in the direction in which disorder increases (146–147).

Hawking argues further that the psychological arrow and the thermodynamic arrow point in the same direction as the expansion of the universe because intelligent beings can only exist in the expanding state. Although the laws of physics do not distinguish between forward and backward directions of time, the thermodynamic arrow, the psychological arrow, and the cosmological arrow all correspond and point in the same direction (152).

Hawking's theory ties the arrows together in a neat package. If there is a thermodynamic arrow and a cosmological arrow, that explains why our psychological arrow is what it is. But we would not have thought of the thermodynamic arrow and the cosmological arrow were it not for the way the human experience of before and after functions. The arrows of physics can be modified or rejected, given future observations. The experience of before and after will never be modified or rejected. And if I am right that the experience of before and after is not an arrow, I think that we should admit that what we call arrows are inventions that have served us well in negotiating our way around the world, but all our theories, both metaphysical and scientific, arise from a base in the experience of before and after. Some of us have gotten used to the idea that time is relativistic, and the consciousness of the flow of time does not correspond to an objective flow of time. That suggests that our science has outstripped the bedrock of human experience. We need to be very wary of anything we think we know about time.

I am suggesting that the psychological experience of time does not require us to maintain the arrows. A world of pure sound with a mind hearing the sound would be a world with no arrow except the so-called psychological arrow which is not an arrow because it does not have a direction. We invent the arrows to make sense of our before-and-after experience. In this book I have argued that given the logic of entailment between past and future, the modal arrow does not make sense. We do not need it anyway. The causal arrow has served us well, and we are probably loath to give it up, but it is confused. Even if a cause is what is before, and an effect is what is after, that is not an arrow. If Hawking is right, the causal arrow is associated with the thermodynamic arrow in that it is much easier to explain the broken pieces of a cup on the floor as caused by a whole cup falling to the floor than to explain the existence of a whole cup caused by the upward movement of pieces of crockery on the floor. The counterfactual arrow can be supported by its similarity to the causal arrow, but it is a tenuous arrow, required by neither science nor metaphysics. One arrow can be supported by another, but if all the arrows depend upon something that is not an arrow, it is a metaphysical leap to call any of them arrows.

What does all this mean for fatalist arguments? If I am right in my previous arguments, fatalists are confused about the arrow at the outset of their argument. Standard fatalist arguments use the necessity of the past, which is half of the modal, causal, or counterfactual arrow of time, in arguing that the given arrow of time does not exist. We are meant to believe that given the accidental necessity of the past, or the causal closure of the past, or the counterfactual fixity of the past, the future is the same as the past. Both are necessary. Fatalist arguments depend upon the intuition of an arrow that allegedly collapses in one direction. The arrow disappears. An unconventional philosopher could have argued the other way. Given the accidental contingency of the future, or the causal openness of the future, or the counterfactual openness of the future, the past is the same as the future. Both are contingent. The thermodynamic arrow of time could explain why we do not think that way even though we could.

A central claim in this book is that fatalist arguments uncover a more serious problem about time. Since the fatalist arguments can be generalized in the ways I have described, the arguments show that we must deny the arrow used in the argument for reasons that have nothing to do with fatalism. The problem is entailment relations between past and future. Fatalist arguments are supposed to show that either we must accept fatalism or we must reject the premise of infallible foreknowledge, causal determinism, or the truth of future contingent propositions. But the logic of these arguments leads to the trilemmas I have described, and that requires giving up much more than the particular premise under discussion. Philosophical arguments sometimes have hidden implications that we overlook to our peril.

Fatalists are confused about time even if they are not guilty of an explicit contradiction in their position on the arrow of time. But to be honest, confusion about time is widespread. In fact, who among us is not confused about time? Is time objectively real? If objective means independent of us, Kant thought that the answer is no. "Time is nothing but the form of inner sense, that is, of the intuition of ourselves and of our inner state.... And just because this inner intuition yields no shape, we endeavour to make up for this want by analogies. We represent the time-sequence by a line progressing to infinity" (1965, B50).

We use analogies all the time, representing one thing by something entirely different and independent of it. We use what we grasp more firmly to help us understand what we grasp more weakly. Analogies are good; I am not opposed to them. But we are sometimes tempted to forget that an analogy is only an analogy. Time does not really have the shape of a line pointing in a certain direction.

I assume that time is an irreducible feature of consciousness. We can surmise what a world of pure time and no space and no perceiver would be like, and I have tried to do that with my excursion into Strawson's fantasy about sound, but if the psychological experience of time is more basic than any of the arrows of time I have mentioned—the modal arrow, the causal arrow, the counterfactual arrow, the thermodynamic arrow, and the cosmic arrow— we are left with the Kantian idea that "Time is nothing but the form of inner sense," the sense of before and after. Is time outside of us real? I hope so, because if it is not, nothing outside of us is real in any form in which I can imagine it.

The reality of time is not the issue for this book, and I am not defending Kant's distinction between the noumenal and phenomenal worlds, but I think that Kant was right that the sense of time is primitive in our consciousness. That is to say, the sense of before and after is primitive; an arrow is not. The problem is that what we think about the arrow of time and what we think about the logical connections between propositions arise from two separated regions of our theoretical reflections, and I have argued that they do not match up. Fatalist arguments are a gift because they reveal a deep problem in our understanding of time and logical entailment. The way we respond to the conflict depends upon which one is firmer in our psychic economy. We can overhaul logic, or we can overhaul the instincts we have about time. Changing logic is something some philosophers are happy to do, but I believe that we should admit that our instincts about time and its arrows are tenuous and based on shaky spatial analogies.

Time is the most fundamental form of our experience, and all our concepts of the internal and external worlds are imbedded in the structure of before and after. We cannot give that up. But I find that in doing philosophy we always have options, and we need to decide what is firmer in the structure of our thought and what is less so. I have not defended the firmness of the belief that there are propositions about the past that entail propositions about the future, and I realize that different readers will have different views about that. But I am convinced that although the experience of before and after is nonnegotiable, the experience of a temporal arrow is not. The belief that we have free will is firm for many of us, but this book is not constructed to attack fatalism. It is about time. The more I contemplate time, the more nebulous it becomes, yet a succession of arguments and thought experiments in this book brings me to an unmistakable conclusion. We say that time is directed toward the future, but the future is not a direction. There is no arrow of time.

Works Cited

Adams, Marilyn. (1967). "Is the Existence of God a 'Hard' Fact?" *Philosophical Review* 76 (October): 492–503.
Alston, William P. (1986). "Does God Have Beliefs?" *Religious Studies* 22: 287–306.
Aquinas, St. Thomas. (2012). *Summa Theologiae*. (Latin and English). Translated by Fr. Laurence Shapcote, OP. Lander, WY: Aquinas Institute for the Study of Sacred Doctrine.
Aristotle. (1941). *Basic Works of Aristotle*. Translated by Richard McKeon.
Back to the Future (film). (1985). Directed by Robert Zemeckis.
Baron, Sam, and Kristie Miller. (2019). *An Introduction to the Philosophy of Time*. Cambridge: Polity Press.
Black, Max. (1956). "Why Cannot an Effect Precede Its Cause." *Analysis* 16: 49–58.
Bobzien, Susanne. (1998). *Determinism and Freedom in Stoic Philosophy*. Oxford: Oxford University Press.
Boethius. (1962). *The Consolation of Philosophy*. Translated by Richard Green. Indianapolis: Bobbs-Merrill Library of Liberal Arts.
Cartwright, Nancy. (1999). *The Dappled World*. Cambridge: Cambridge University Press.
Church, Alonzo. (1996) *Introduction to Mathematical Logic*. Princeton Landmarks in Mathematics. Reprint edition. Princeton: Princeton University Press.
Craig, William. (1990). *Divine Foreknowledge and Human Freedom*. Brill's Studies in Intellectual History 19. Leiden: E.J. Brill.
Dekker, Eef. (2000). *Middle Knowledge*. Leuven: Peeters.
Dummett, Michael. (1964). "Bringing About the Past." *Philosophical Review* 73: 338–359.
Dupré, J. (2001). *Human Nature and the Limits of Science*. Oxford: Oxford University Press.
Epictetus. (2008). *Discourses and Selected Writings*. Translated and edited by Robert Dobbin. London: Penguin Classics.
Finch, Alicia, and Michael Rea. (2008). "Presentism and Ockham's Way Out." In *Oxford Studies in Philosophy of Religion*, vol. 1, ed. Jonathan Kvanvig. Oxford: Oxford University Press, 1–17.
Finch, Alicia, and Ted Warfield. (1998). "The *MIND* Argument and Libertarianism." *Mind* 107, no. 427 (July): 515–528. doi:10.1093/mind/107.427.515.
Fischer, John Martin. (1983). "Freedom and Foreknowledge." *Philosophical Review* 92 (January): 67–79.
Fischer, John Martin. (1984). "Power over the Past." *Pacific Philosophical Quarterly* 65, no. 4: 335–350. Reprinted in Fischer (2016), chapter 5.

Fischer, John Martin, ed. (1989). *God, Foreknowledge, and Freedom.* Stanford, CA: Stanford University Press.

Fischer, John Martin. (1994). *The Metaphysics of Free Will.* Oxford and Malden, MA: Wiley-Blackwell.

Fischer, John Martin. (2011a). "Foreknowledge, Freedom, and the Fixity of the Past." *Philosophia* 39: 461–474. Reprinted in Fischer (2016), chapter 6.

Fischer, John Martin. (2011b). "Putting Molinism in Its Place." In *Molinism: The Contemporary Debate*, ed. Ken Perzyck. Oxford: Oxford University Press, 208–226. Reprinted in Fischer (2016), chapter 4.

Fischer, John Martin. (2016). *Our Fate: Essays on God and Free Will.* New York: Oxford University Press.

Fischer, John Martin, and Patrick Todd, eds. (2015). *Freedom, Fatalism, and Foreknowledge.* New York: Oxford University Press.

Flint, Thomas. (1998). *Divine Providence: The Molinist Account.* Ithaca, NY: Cornell University Press.

Freddoso, Alfred. (1983). "Accidental Necessity and Logical Determinism." *Journal of Philosophy* 80, no. 5: 257–278.

Hasker, William. (1989). *God, Time, and Knowledge.* Ithaca, NY: Cornell University Press.

Hawking, Stephen. (1988). *A Brief History of Time.* New York: Bantam Books.

Hoefer, Carl. (2023). "Causal Determinism." In *The Stanford Encyclopedia of Philosophy* (Spring 2023 edition), ed. Edward N. Zalta and Uri Nodelman. Stanford University. https://plato.stanford.edu/archives/spr2023/entries/determinism-causal/.

Hume, David. (2000). *A Treatise of Human Nature.* Edited by Mary J. Norton and David F. Norton. Oxford: Oxford University Press.

Hunt, David. (1998). "What *Is* the Problem of Theological Fatalism?" *International Philosophical Quarterly* 37: 1, 17–30.

Hunt, David P. (2020). "Fatalism for Presentists." In *The Metaphysics of Time: Themes on Prior*, ed. Per Hasle, David Jakobsen, and Peter Ohstrom. Aalborg, Denmark: Aalborg University Press, 299–316.

Interstellar (film). (2014). Directed by Christopher Nolan.

Kant, Immanuel. (1965). *A Critique of Pure Reason.* Translated by Norman Kemp Smith. New York: St. Martin's Press.

Kvanvig, Jonathan. (1986). *The Possibility of an All-Knowing God.* New York: St. Martin's Press.

Lang, Andrew. (2022). *The Brown Fairy Book.* Amanda Publishing (independent). http://mythfolklore.net/andrewlang/260.htm.

Lewis, David. (1981). "Am I Free to Break the Laws?" *Theoria* 47: 112–121.

Maugham, W. Somerset. (2007). *Maugham Plays.* Vol. 1. London: A&C Black.

Mavrodes, George. (1984). "Is the Past Unpreventable?" *Faith and Philosophy* 1, no. 2 (April): 131–146.

McKay, Thomas J., and David Johnson. (1996). "A Reconsideration of an Argument Against Compatibilism." *Philosophical Topics* 2, no. 2: 113–122. doi:10.5840/philtopics199624219.

Molina, Luis de. (1988). *On Divine Foreknowledge* (Part IV of the *Concordia*). Translation and introduction by Alfred J. Freddoso. Ithaca, NY: Cornell University Press.

Nozick, Robert. (1969). "Newcomb's Problem and Two Principles of Choice." In *Essays in Honor of Carl G. Hempel*, ed. Nicholas Rescher. Dordrecht: Reidel, 114–146.

O'Connor, Timothy. (1993). "On the Transfer of Necessity." *Noûs* 27, no. 2: 204–218. doi:10.2307/2215756.

Pereboom, Derk. (2006). *Living Without Free Will*. Cambridge Studies in Philosophy. Cambridge: Cambridge University Press.

Perry, John, (2004). "Compatibilist Options." In *Freedom and Determinism*, ed. J. Campbell, M. O'Rourke, and D. Shier. Cambridge, MA: MIT Press, 231–254.

Pike, Nelson. (1993). "A Latter-Day Look at the Foreknowledge Problem." *International Journal for Philosophy of Religion* 33, no. 3 (June): 129–164.

Plantinga, Alvin. (1986). "On Ockham's Way Out." *Faith and Philosophy* 3, no. 3 (July): 235–269.

Prior, A. N. (1962). "The Formalities of Omniscience." *Philosophy* 37 (April): 114–129. Reprinted in Per Hasle, Peter Øhrstøm, Torben Braüner, and Jack Copeland, eds. *Papers on Time and Tense*. New edition. Oxford: Oxford University Press, 2003, 39–58.

Rice, Hugh. (2005). "Zagzebski on the Arrow of Time." *Faith and Philosophy* 22, no. 3: 363–369.

Helmut Schoeck. (1966). *Envy: A Theory of Social Behaviour*. Indianapolis: Liberty Fund.

Sobel, Jordan Howard. (1998). *Puzzles for the Will*. Toronto: University of Toronto Press.

Sophocles. (2022). *Oedipus Rex*. Translated by Francis Storr. Independently published.

Strawson, Peter. (1959). *Individuals: An Essay in Descriptive Metaphysics*. London: Routledge.

Todd, Patrick. (2021). *The Open Future: Why Future Contingents Are All False*. Oxford: Oxford University Press.

Van Fraassen, Bas. (1989). *Laws and Symmetry*. Oxford: Clarendon Press.

Van Inwagen, Peter. (1983). *An Essay on Free Will*. Oxford: Clarendon Press.

Van Inwagen, Peter. (2000). "Free Will Remains a Mystery." *Philosophical Perspectives* 14: 1–20.

Vihvilen, Kahdri. (2022). "Arguments for Incompatibilism." In *The Stanford Encyclopedia of Philosophy* (Fall 2022 edition), ed. Edward N. Zalta and Uri Nodelman. Standford University. https://plato.stanford.edu/archives/fall2022/entries/incompatibilism-arguments/.

Warfield, Ted. (2000). "Causal Determinism and Human Freedom Are Incompatible: A New Argument for Incompatibilism." *Philosophical Perspectives* 14: 167–180.

Wasserman, Ryan. (2021). "Freedom, Foreknowledge, and Dependence." *Noûs* 55, no. 3: 603–622.

Widerker, David. (1990). "Troubles with Ockhamism." *Journal of Philosophy* 87, no. 9: 462–480.

WORKS CITED

Wierenga, Edward. (1989). *The Nature of God*. Ithaca, NY: Cornell University Press.

William of Ockham. (1983). *Predestination, God's Foreknowledge, and Future Contingents*. 2nd ed. Translated with introduction and notes by Marilyn McCord Adams and Norman Kretzmann. Indianapolis: Hackett.

Zagzebski, Linda. (1991). *The Dilemma of Freedom and Foreknowledge*. New York: Oxford University Press.

Zagzebski, Linda. (2011). "Eternity and Fatalism." In *God, Eternity, and Time*, ed. C. Tapp and E. Runggaldier. Farnham, UK and Burlington, VT: Ashgate Press, 65–80. Reprinted in Zagzebski (2022), chapter 2.

Zagzebski, Linda. (2014). "Divine Foreknowledge and the Metaphysics of Time." In *God, Reason, and Reality*, ed. Anselm Ramelow. *Philosophia* series: Basic Philosophical Concepts. Munich: Philosophia Verlag, 275–302. Reprinted in Zagzebski (2022), chapter 3.14.

Zagzebski, Linda. (2017). "Foreknowledge and Free Will." In *Stanford Encyclopedia of Philosophy*, ed. Edward Zalta. Stanford University. Revised by David Hunt 2021. https://plato.stanford.edu/archives/sum2022/entries/free-will-foreknowledge/.

Zagzebski, Linda. (2022). *God, Knowledge, and the Good: Collected Papers in Philosophy of Religion*. New York: Oxford University Press.

Index

For the benefit of digital users, indexed terms that span two pages (e.g., 52–53) may, on occasion, appear on only one of those pages.

accidental necessity
   incoherence of, 52–56
   Ockhamism and, 20–25, 35, 41, 52–56
   soft and hard forms of past and, 30, 46, 47–48, 54, 60–61, 109
   theological fatalism and, 14–15, 17–18, 20–25, 30, 34–35, 37, 38, 40–61
   Transfer of Accidental Necessity principle, 15–16, 25, 27–51
   See also necessity of the past
act/potency distinction, 20–21, 23, 24, 27, 56
Adams, Marilyn, 13–14, 21n.5, 22–23, 46n.16
Aeneas, 1–2
Alston, William P., 28–29, 30
alternative possibilities. *See* Principle of Alternate Possibilities (PAP)
Appointment with Death (legend in Somerset Maugham), 2
Aquinas, Thomas
   divine foreknowledge and, 12–13, 28–29, 30
   future contingents and, 13
   theological fatalism and, 12–13, 28–29, 30
   Thomistic Ockhamism and, 30
   timelessness of God and, 28
Aristotle
   act/potency distinction and, 20–21, 49, 56
   arrow of time and, 52
   logical fatalism rejected by, 49
   necessity of the past and, 56–57
   Sea Battle arguments and, 12, 49–50

   terminology of, 24
   universal fatalism rejected by, 5–6
arrow of time
   backward agent causation and, 92–93, 101–2
   causal arrow of time, 64, 82, 83, 85, 105, 106
   cosmological arrow of time, 117
   counterfactual arrow of time, 101–2, 104–5, 118–19
   determinism and, 84–85
   fatalist use of, 37–38, 52–53, 57–58, 118–21
   Fixed Past Constraint and, 101–2
   modal arrow of time, 37–38, 52–53, 54–55, 105–6
   nature of time and, 114–16
   necessity of the past and, 56, 59
   Ockhamism and, 55–56, 100
   plausibility of, 112–21
   psychological arrow of time, 91–96, 105–6, 110, 112–13, 115–17, 118
   thermodynamic arrow of time, 60–61, 116–18, 119–20
   trilemmas involving, 82–86
   world of pure sound and, 114–16, 118
Augustine, 12–13

backward agent causation, 86–99, 101–2
Berkeley, George, 114
Big Fated Event, 1–2, 3
Bilking argument, 93–94
Black, Max, 93
Boethius, 3–6, 12–13, 28

Calvinist predestination, 33–34

128 INDEX

causal fatalism
  arrow of time and, 64, 82, 83, 85, 105, 106
  causal closure-based argument for, 63-78, 107-8
  causal modality distinguished from temporal modality and, 21-22
  definition of, 7
  definition of causal closure and, 65-66
  determinism and, 85, 108-9
  free will and, 85, 108-9
  Ockhamism and, 109-10
  overview of, 7
  PAP and, 39, 68, 78, 109
  short argument for, 8-10
  timelessness of God and, 108-9
  Transfer of Causal Closure Principle and, 65, 66, 67, 68-70, 71, 79
  unpreventability of the past-based argument for, 73-74
causal loops, 32-33, 87, 98
Church, Alonzo, 79n.1
Consolation of Philosophy, The (Boethius), 3-4
counterfactual arrow of time. *See* arrow of time

De Interpretatione (Aristotle), 12
Dekker, Eef, 29n.9
determinism
  arrow of time and, 84-85
  backward causation and, 98-99
  causal fatalism and, 85, 108-9
  consequences argument against, 71-72, 76-86, 106
  fatalism's relation to, 3, 39, 78, 107-8
  forms of argument for, 79-80
  free will and, 10, 39, 71-72, 76-86, 106-7
  incompatibilism and, 71-72, 76-86, 106
  necessity of the past and, 8-9n.3, 38, 44, 65, 78-87, 109
  Ockhamism and, 47
  PAP and, 80, 81-82, 109
  theological fatalism and, 47-48
Diodorus Cronus, 12

divine foreknowledge. *See* theological fatalism
Dummett, Michael, 88-94, 96-97, 99-100

Epictetus, 12

fatalism
  acceptance of, 5-6
  ancient interest in, 1
  Big Fated Event form of, 1-3
  definition of, 1-3
  destiny's relation to, 1-2
  determinism's relation to, 3, 9-10, 39, 78, 107-8
  forms of, 1-3, 7-10
  free will and, 5-6
  Greek anxiety over fate and, 4-5
  mythological understanding of, 1-3
  negative reaction in history to, 5-6
  overview of, 1-10
  personification of, 3-5
  plausibility of, 6, 7-10
  scientific research on accepting fate and, 4
  short arguments for, 7-10
  structure of current volume on, 10
  universal form of, 3, 5-7
  wheel of fortune and, 3-4
  See also causal fatalism; logical fatalism; theological fatalism
Fischer, John Martin, 9n.4, 29n.10, 32n.12, 33n.13, 45, 99nn.9-10, 107-8
Fixed Past Constraint (FPC), 99, 100-2
Flint, Thomas, 29nn.9-10
Freddoso, Alfred, 29n.10
free will
  causal fatalism and, 85, 108-9
  consequence argument and, 71-72, 76-86, 106
  determinism and, 10, 39, 71-72, 76-86, 106-7
  fatalism's relation to, 5-6
  incompatibilism and, 71-72, 76-86, 106
  necessity of the past and, 78-86

INDEX 129

Ockhamism and, 47, 109–10
PAP and, 53–54, 80, 81–82, 109
theological fatalism and, 11–13, 25–34, 38–39, 45–46, 105

God. *See* theological fatalism

Hasker, William, 29n.10
Hawking, Stephen, 116–17
Hume, David, 88, 109–10
Hunt, David, 9n.4, 25n.6

incompatibilism, 71–72, 76–86, 106
infallibility. *See* theological fatalism

Job 1:21, 4
Johnson, David, 80n.3

Kant, Immanuel, 113, 114, 119–20

Lewis, David, 81n.4, 109–10
Living Without Free Will (Pereboom), 5–6
logical fatalism
  definition of, 7
  future contingents and, 50–51
  historical development of, 11–14
  Master Argument and, 12–13
  modal logical entailments and, 12–13
  necessity of the past and, 12–13, 14, 65–66, 108
  Ockhamism and, 22, 108, 109–10
  overview of, 7
  PAP and, 67, 73
  short argument for, 7, 49
  theological fatalism's relation to, 17–18
  time and, 108–9
  timelessness of God and, 108–9
  Transfer of Accidental Necessity principle and, 49–51
  Transfer of Unpreventability Principle and, 73
  truth and necessity distinction and, 50–51
  unpreventability of the past argument for, 73

Master Argument for fatalism, 12

Mavrodes, George, 96
McKay, Thomas, 80n.3
Middle Knowledge, 29
modal arrow of time. *See* arrow of time
Molinism, 29

necessity and truth distinction, 22, 50–51, 59, 108
necessity of the past
  act/potency distinction and, 20–21
  arrow of time and, 56, 59
  backward agent causation and, 86–98
  Bilking argument and, 93–94
  causal closure of the past and, 63–78
  causal modality distinguished from temporal modality and, 21–22
  confusion about, 15
  contingency of the future and, 35
  counterfactual power over the past and, 98–106
  definition of causal closure and, 65–66
  determinism and, 8–9n.3, 38, 44, 65, 76–87, 109
  Fixed Past Constraint and, 99–101
  free will and, 78–86
  incoherence of accidental necessity and, 52–56
  logical fatalism and, 12–13, 14, 65–66, 108
  necessity *per accidens,* 13–14, 34–35, 56, 63
  Newcomb puzzle and, 31, 33–34, 90–91, 93, 110
  non-causability of the past principle and, 70
  now-necessity, 14
  Ockhamism and, 13–14, 109–10
  PAP and, 78
  real modalities and, 23–24
  revisiting of, 63–86
  Rule Beta and, 80–82, 83–84
  soft and hard forms of past and, 109
  theological fatalism and, 12, 19–20, 35, 94–95, 102–3, 107–8, 109
  Transfer of Accidental Necessity principle and, 15–16, 25
  Transfer of Counterfactual Power Principle and, 101

necessity of the past (*cont.*)
  Transfer of non-causability principle and, 70–71, 75, 82, 97
  Transfer of Unpreventability Principle and, 73
  trilemmas faced by arguments for, 82–86, 97–98
  truth and necessity distinction and, 22
  unpreventability of the past principle and, 71–73, 75, 77–78, 83, 84, 107–8
  See also accidental necessity; arrow of time
Newcomb puzzle, 31, 33–34, 90–91, 93, 110
non-causability of the past principle, 70
Nozick, Robert, 31n.11

Ockhamism
  accidental necessity and, 20–25, 35, 41, 52–56
  act/potency distinction and, 39–40
  arrow of time and, 55–56, 100
  causal fatalism and, 109–10
  causal modality distinguished from temporal modality and, 21–22
  counterfactual power version of, 104–5, 109–10
  defenses of, 48n.18
  determinism and, 47, 109
  free will and, 47, 109–10
  incoherence of accidental necessity and, 52–56
  logical fatalism and, 22, 108, 109–10
  necessity of the past and, 13–14, 109–10
  necessity *per accidens* and, 13–14, 34–35, 56, 63
  now-necessity and, 14
  real modalities and, 23–24
  soft and hard forms of past and, 30, 46, 47–48, 54, 60–61, 109
  theological fatalism and, 20–25, 30, 53
  Thomistic Ockhamism, 30, 53
  truth and necessity distinction and, 22, 50–51

O'Connor, Timothy, 80n.3
Oedipus Rex (Sophocles), 2

past, necessity of. *See* necessity of the past
Pereboom, Derek, 5–6
Plantinga, Alvin, 100–3, 104–5, 109–10
Plato, 69
potency/act distinction, 20–21, 23, 24, 27, 56
predestination, 33–34, 59
Principle of Alternate Possibilities (PAP)
  causal fatalism and, 39, 68, 78, 109
  definition of, 16
  denial of, 39, 53–54
  determinism and, 80, 81–82, 109
  free will and, 80, 81–82, 109
  logical fatalism and, 67, 73
  theological fatalism and, 17, 39, 53–54
principles. *See* non-causability of the past principle; Principle of Alternate Possibilities (PAP); Transfer of Accidental Necessity principle; Transfer of Causal Closure Principle; Transfer of Counterfactual Power Principle; Transfer of non-causability principle; Transfer of Unpreventability Principle; unpreventability of the past principle
psychological arrow of time. *See* arrow of time

Rule Beta, 71–72, 79–82, 83–84, 98, 99–100

Schoeck, Helmut, 4
Sea Battle arguments, 12, 49–50
Sheppey (Maugham), 2n.2
Sobel, Howard, 33n.13
soft and hard forms of past, 30, 46, 46n.16, 47–48, 54, 60–61, 109
standard fatalist arguments. *See* causal fatalism; fatalism; logical fatalism; theological fatalism
Stoicism, 12–13
Strawson, Peter, 113

INDEX 131

theological fatalism
  accidental necessity and, 14–15, 17–18, 20–25, 30, 34–35, 37, 38, 40–61
  avoiding the conclusion and, 56–61
  belief states, God as lacking, 28–29
  bi-directionality and, 47
  Calvinist predestination and, 33–34
  causal loops and, 33
  causal modality distinguished from temporal modality and, 21–22
  core argument for, 16–17
  definition of, 7
  determinism and, 47–48
  divine infallibility and, 17–19, 25–52, 72–73
  free will and, 11–13, 25–34, 38–39, 45–46, 105
  future contingents and, 13
  historical development of, 11–14
  incoherence of accidental necessity and, 52–56
  infallibility's relation to fatalism and, 34–40
  infallibility's relation to God's knowledge and, 25–34
  infallibility's relation to time and, 40–52
  invalid arguments for, 17–20
  logical fatalism's relation to, 17–18
  Middle Knowledge and, 29
  Molinism and, 29
  necessity of the past and, 12, 19–20, 35, 94–95, 102–3, 107–8, 109
  Newcomb puzzle and, 31–34
  Ockhamism and, 20–25, 30, 53
  Open Theism and, 39–40
  overview of, 7, 61–62
  PAP and, 17, 39, 53–54
  pre-Christian foreshadowing of, 12–13
  primary argument for, 11–20
  proposed solutions to, 27–34, 52–56
  reactions to and consequences of arguments on, 56–61
  real modalities and, 23–24
  relation to other forms of fatalism, 45–46
  short argument for, 7–8
  soft and hard forms of past and, 46–48, 54
  Thomistic Ockhamism and, 30, 53
  timelessness of God solution to, 28, 108–9
  time travel and, 87
  Transfer of Accidental Necessity principle and, 49–51
  truth and necessity distinction and, 22
  unpreventability of the past argument for, 72–73
  unraveling of, 25–56
Thomas Aquinas. *See* Aquinas, Thomas
time
  causal closure of the past and, 63–78
  definition of causal closure and, 65–66
  timelessness of God, 28, 108–9
  time travel, 87, 96
  See also arrow of time; necessity of the past
Todd, Patrick, 9n.4, 51n.19
Transfer of Accidental Necessity principle, 15–16, 25, 49–51
Transfer of Causal Closure Principle, 65, 66, 67, 68–70, 71, 79
Transfer of Counterfactual Power Principle, 101
Transfer of non-causability principle, 70–71, 75, 82, 97
Transfer of Unpreventability Principle, 71–72, 73, 74–75, 83
truth and necessity distinction, 22, 50–51, 59, 108

unpreventability of the past principle, 71–73, 75, 77–78, 83, 84, 107–8

van Inwagen, Peter, 71–72, 78–80, 99–100
Vihvilen, Kadri, 80n.2

Warfield, Ted, 85n.5
Wasserman, Ryan, 96
William of Ockham, 12–14. *See also* Ockhamism

Zagzebski, Linda, 60n.20